The Mathews Collection

featuring McLaren, Ferrari, Corvette & other important marques

by William Taylor

Coterie Press Limited

THE MATHEWS COLLECTION
Featuring McLaren, Ferrari, Corvette & other important marques

A COTERIE PRESS BOOK

First British Edition July 2001

Published in the UK by Coterie Press Limited

6 Forest Hill Industrial Estate, Perry Vale, Forest Hill, London SE23 2LX

Tel: +44 (0)20 8699 5111

coterieltd@aol.com

For other books by Coterie Press have a look at **www.lotusbook.com**

ISBN : 1 902351 02 9

The Authors extend their special thanks for help in the preparation of this book to : Harry & Cris Mathews, his son Greg, daughter Pamela, son-in-law Mark and everyone else at the Mathews Collection. For contact details and further information on the Mathews Collection try their website at **www.mathewscollection.com**

BY: **WILLIAM TAYLOR**

WORDS BY: **ZOE HARDINGE**

CREATIVE DIRECTOR: **WILLIAM TAYLOR**

EDITOR: **JAMES BENNETT**

DESIGN: **PAUL COOPER**

PRINTED BY : **COLORPRINT**: Hong Kong

ORIGINATION BY : **GLOBAL COLOUR**: Malaysia

ALL COMMISSIONED PHOTOGRAPHY BY WILLIAM TAYLOR additional photographs courtesy of Dave Friedman, Gordon L. Jolley & Jim Bennett

Contents

Introduction *by Harry Mathews*

My first sports car was a 1953 Jaguar Xk120 roadster that I purchased for $795 in 1959. The Collection started in the late 70's when I acquired about 20 cars - Porsche, Ferrari, Mercedes 300SL, Jaguar. I have driven various brands of sports cars ever since but my preference now leans to Italian and German cars.

After years of racing off-road motorcycles, I started entering track events in 1978 in my Porsche 928. In 1984, I began vintage road racing with a Lotus 51 Formula Ford which cost $3500. In 1987, my son Greg, became interested in racing and shortly after that my daughter, Pamela, also started racing. With Pam's marriage to Mark Burgard, a fourth race car driver was acquired. We've been racing as a family ever since.

In 1987, we entered a race at Road America in Elkhart Lake, Wisconsin and while there, I saw a 1967 McLaren-Elva M1-C for sale. I purchased that car and my interest in McLarens began. In 1989 we purchased our second McLaren, the M8-D.

McLaren were very successful in Can-Am/Group 7, Formula One, Formula 5000, and at the Indy 500. McLaren cars won the Can-Am Championship five years in a row 1967-1971, with Bruce winning his first Can-Am title in 1967 at the wheel of the all new M6-A. I now have the honor of owning and driving this exceptional piece of motorsports history. The M-16 series of Indy cars were successful all through the 1970's. McLaren also ran Formula One and Formula 5000 all at the same time. Bruce's secret of success was thorough testing and attention to detail. He came ready to race while many competitors did their testing at the race, meeting with poor results most of the time.

I never personally met Bruce McLaren, but I was fortunate to meet Denny Hulme at Road America in 1992 just a few months before he died. In 1967 I had seen both of them race in the Can-Am at Road America. At that time I never dreamed that 30 years later, I would have the honor of helping to keep their legacy and incredible racing history alive through the stewardship of all these fabulous cars. There is such an aura of history surrounding them. I saw them race at Elkhart lake and it's ironic; one of the cars I own is the M6A that bruce won the championship with in 1967. I have raced that car at Elkhart Lake for the last four years on the same track that I saw Bruce race on. I have better tires and more horsepower, but I still haven't gotten down to his lap times. I have also been fortunate enough to meet the members of Bruce's family who operate the Bruce McLaren Trust and am indebted to them for their help and advice.

All of our McLarens are fully operational and most are race ready. We always attend the Can-Am feature race held at Road America every year in July. It gives fans and potential customers a chance to see the McLarens in action at a track where they originally raced. It is certainly the most beautiful track in all of North America and the event in July is very special.

I started Vintage Sales in 1985, which is a licensed Colorado vehicle dealer, for the purpose of buying and selling sports cars, race cars, and collector cars. Over the last 16 years, we have built a worldwide reputation as a reliable source of top quality collector cars. Our speciality, one in which we are recognized as being one of the top authorities in the world, is vintage McLaren racecars. In addition to the McLarens, the collection also includes beautifully restored examples of high performance sports cars, customs, and hot rods.

Harry Mathews

HARRY MATHEWS

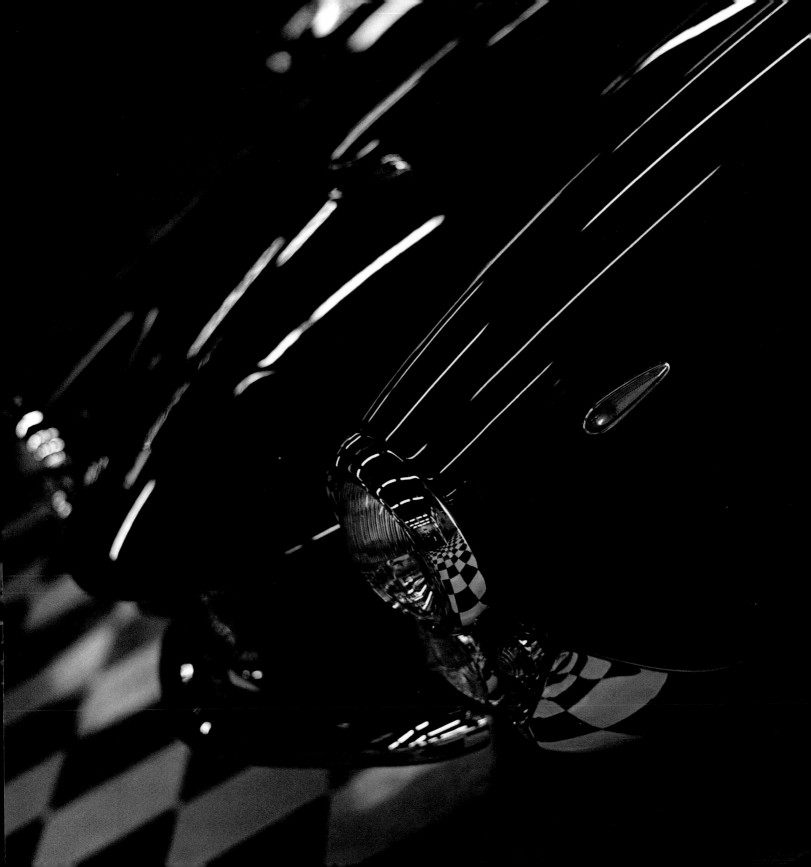

Foreword *by Brian Redman*

It is a delight to read this beautifully written and produced book by William Taylor and his team at Coterie Press.

With it's special emphasis on the legendary McLarens, the Harry Mathews collection of racing cars is one of the best in the world. These cars do not sit, gathering dust, instead, they are put to the use that Bruce and his talented team of designers, engineers and drivers intended - racing on America's finest road racing circuits, driven by Harry and his family.

Through this book, we can live again the glory that was Can-Am. Unlimited power, noise, color, great drivers. If you're in the Arvada area, be sure to call in and see the wonderful collection of cars at Nostalgia Racing.

BRIAN REDMAN.

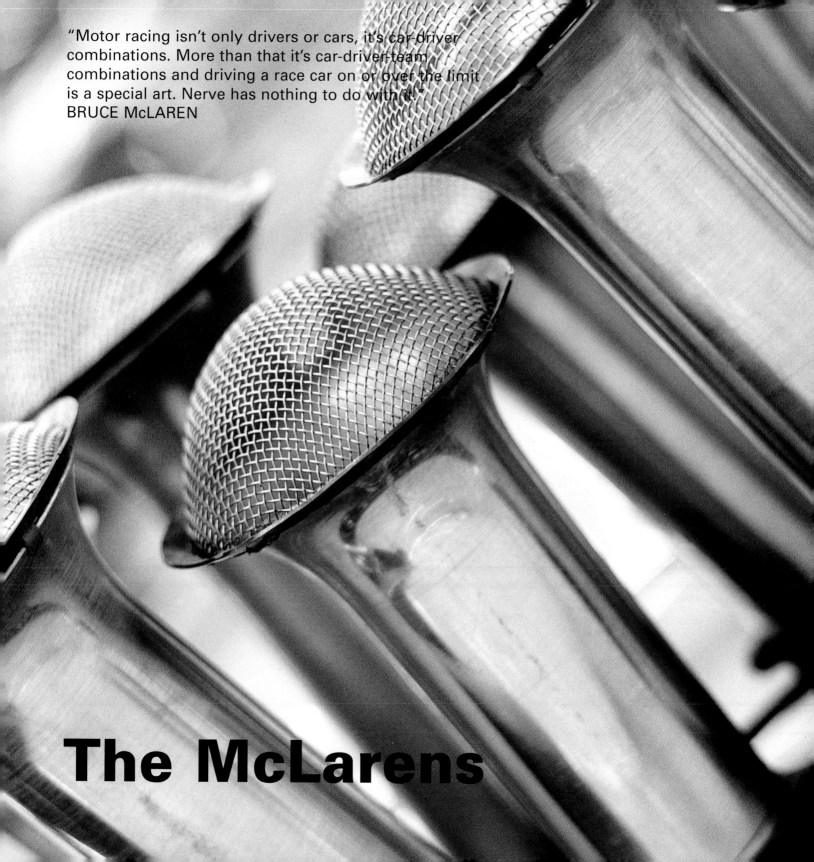

"Motor racing isn't only drivers or cars, it's car-driver combinations. More than that it's car-driver-team combinations and driving a race car on or over the limit is a special art. Nerve has nothing to do with it."
BRUCE McLAREN

The McLarens

McLaren-Elva M1A

" The first customer car from McLaren "

Team McLaren was started by Bruce McLaren late in 1963. Bruce wanted to race two of his own 'Cooper Specials' in the Tasman series planned for Australia and his native New Zealand. The 'Cooper Specials' were modifications of the car he was driving for the Cooper Formula One Team at the time. Bruce made the two chassis slimmer and lighter and, with the help of Teddy Mayer, acquired Coventry Climax engines to run in them.

'Bruce McLaren Motor Racing Ltd' tested their prototype 'Cooper Special' in September 1963 and entered their first race at Levin, New Zealand on the 4th January 1964. In his own country, under his own banner and in his first race Bruce's cars came first and second, quite an achievement. Bruce was extremely encouraged; he had applied his own principles to racing and won.

McLaren needed to decide in which direction he was going to take his team and with an eye to lucrative sports car racing, he bought Roger Penske's 'Zerex Special'. The 'Zerex Special' was a controversial choice, it was already pushing at the limits of the SCCA rules since it was little more than a wide bodied Grand Prix Cooper still with its original central seating position. After the success of the Zerex Special, the SCCA clarified their rules, stating that to be classed as a sportscar, the car must have two seating positions, one either side of the car's central line.

McLaren created his 'Cooper-Oldsmobile' by replacing the Zerex's 4-cylinder 2.7 litre Coventry Climax engine with a larger, yet lighter, Oldsmobile 3.9 litre aluminum engine. He also scrapped the entire central section of the Zerex chassis, replacing it with a tubular frame of his own design. The Cooper Oldsmobile won first time out with McLaren behind the wheel in the 1964 Players 200 at Mosport, Ontario, Canada, an event that was a forerunner to the Can Am series.

From this victorious start the decision was made to build the

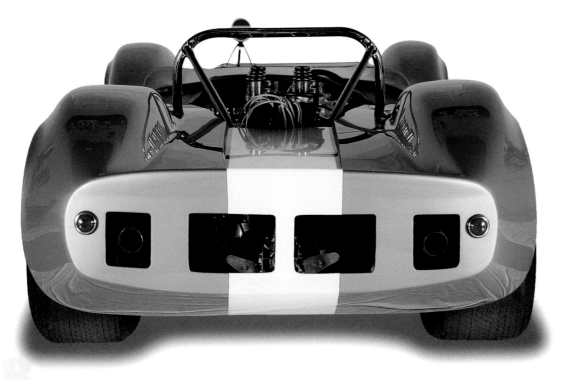

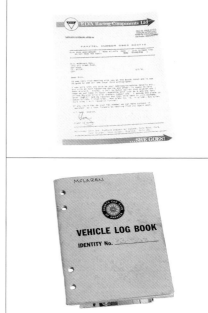

first real McLaren from Bruce's own designs. In September 1964 the new McLaren-Oldsmobile started testing at Goodwood. The Mark 1 was a simple space frame design of round and square tubing with light alloy sheeting rivetted and bonded to form a stressed and bonded undertray. The Mark 1 was fitted with an Oldsmobile V8 engine, Cooper wheels, uprights and steering arms, and a 4-speed Hewland gearbox. The new car had its racing debut at Mosport Park that September and was the fastest car on the track until a throttle linkage broke incurring a long pit stop which resulted in Bruce finishing third. The Mark 1 was soon setting records on the American circuits and with the success came requests from other drivers who wanted replicas.

Team McLaren had considered putting the Mark 1 into limited production, but as the "factory" only consisted of seven men it was decided that it was well beyond their means, both financially and logistically. Frank Nichols of Elva Cars Ltd, a small speciality car maker based in Rye, England, went to see Team McLaren and suggested building customer McLarens on a royalty per car basis.

A deal was struck and an association was formed with Peter Agg of Trojan (Elva's financial backers) to build McLaren racing replicas. In November 1964 the M1A went into production as the McLaren-Elva Mark 1. Work began immediately on twenty four customer M1As in order to have a car on display at the London racing car show in January 1965.

The M1A chassis was formed of a large diameter round and

SPECIFICATIONS

Make: McLaren-Elva	Model: M1-A
Year: 1965	Color: Gold and white
Engine: Chevrolet V8	CC: 5645
Power: 400 bhp	Transmission: ZF 5 speed
Brakes: Girling Discs	Length: 166"
Width: 64"	Height: 51"
Weight: 1828 lbs	Chassis no: 20-01
Drivers: Graham Hill, Elvis Presley	

square tubular frame, the same as the McLaren-Oldsmobile, but the strength was improved by bonding and rivetting the magnesium panels to the cockpit as well. The body design was improved from the original McLaren-Oldsmobile by stylist Tony Hilder, but building problems began as soon as production did.

Elva had nothing to work from - the Mark 1 was in America racing and no design drawings existed. The main stumbling block this caused was for the body, the M1A was to be built from fiberglass copies cast from the original hand formed and beaten alloy body of the Mark 1. The lack of any form of reference drove Elva to build a body mould from the only photographs available to them, but upon his return to England, Bruce found the mould was not completely to his liking and

changes were made which can be seen in later M1As.

The car in the Mathews collection is the first of the Elva built cars, chassis 20-01, and is the car that premiered at the London Racing Car Show, the first McLaren customer car the world had ever seen. The car was then bought by John Coombs, a Jaguar dealer in England, for Graham Hill to drive using a 4.5 litre Oldsmobile engine. The 1965 British sportscar season started at Silverstone on March 20th. The weather was typical for England in spring and the torrential rain did not stop, causing the sportscar race to be called off after 18 of the 25 laps. Graham Hill, in the M1A, found his engine had drowned out, refusing to run on both banks of cylinders at the same time. Hill also drove the M1A at the Los Angeles Times Grand Prix in October 1965. He was running in third when the wheel studs broke on the left rear wheel sending him into the wall. After the race, John Coombs sold the

car to Jerry Entin, a California racer. The M1A's new owner landed it a part in the movie 'Spinout', in which Elvis Presley drove the car.

The Mathews M1A has had a long and eventful history. It is not only the first ever production McLaren, the first ever seen by the public, one with a long and eventful racing history but it was also driven by one of the greatest rock and roll stars of all time. The car is one of only five or six remaining M1As and is most certainly the most original, boasting the spare wheel still strangely located ahead of the dashboard and behind the windscreen.

In June 2000 the Mathews M1A was invited by Lord March of England to appear in a tribute to Bruce McLaren at the

Goodwood Festival of Speed hillclimb. The M1A along with The Mathews M6A, were shipped over to England and with Harry driving the latter, Lord March asked if he could have the honor of driving the M1A up the hill during the weekend.

The event took place in the picturesque grounds of Goodwood House, Sussex and with the British weather giving one of its better showings, both cars performed equally faultlessly over the three days. The M1A was driven in the hillclimb event by Lord March in his usual assured manner and, during the tribute parades on both days, he had the pleasure of being chauffeur to Jan McLaren-Storr (Bruce's sister) who had travelled over to Europe specially for the event. Jan and her husband John run the Bruce McLaren Trust from their base in New Zealand and are actively involved in furthering the historical archives relating to Bruce and all the McLaren cars.

The 30th Anniversary tribute to Bruce McLaren saw the appearance of several rarely seen but very significant McLaren cars. In addition to bringing the current McLaren Mercedes MP4/14 Formula 1 car driven by Nick Heidfeld, McLaren International also brought along two other F1 cars from their extensive collection; a 1969 M7C and a 1985 MP4/2. Other single seaters seen were The Donington Collection's 1969 M9A, Ean Pugh's 1969 M10, David Coplowe's 1967 M4A and Graham Wilcox's 1970 M14A. CanAm cars were seen from the collections of Chuck Haines with his 1969 M8B reconstruction and Robert Horne's 1970 M8D. There were also McLaren F1s to be seen from Chris Palmer with a standard road version and Nick Mason in his 1995 6.0 Litre F1GTR Le Mans car, with a total of 13 cars, all in all quite a selection.

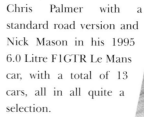

McLaren-Elva M1B

The M1B was the McLaren team car for 1965 through to 1966, as well as the McLaren-Elva customer car for 1966. Elva announced they would be building the M1B in September 1965; it was the second car to be produced by Elva, but the first to be successful for both works and customer drivers, in England and America (where the M1B was sold as the McLaren-Elva Mark 2). In total, Elva produced twenty eight M1B's.

The design was based on the M1A, with engineer Robin Herd retaining and revising the frame to make it 20% stronger without gaining any weight. The strength was gained by using larger diameter round and square mild steel tubes stiffened by sheet alloy rivetted and bonded to it, forming the undertrays and bulkheads. The M1B body was designed by English motor sport artist Michael Turner. He also created the Team McLaren badge, using an image of the Kiwi, the iconic New Zealand flightless bird. Turner designed the M1B body using very strict guidelines laid down by Bruce, including a rigid set of cross sections and aerodynamic requirements. After the final drawings were made, a model was built for wind tunnel testing to improve lines and streamlining. Much attention was paid to lift and drag characteristics,. The M1B's front end was blunt, shaped like the Penske Zerex, to try and eliminate the uplift that had been apparent with the more wing shaped M1A. A clear Plexiglass spoiler was also added to the rear of the M1B to help with downforce.

Bruce drove the prototype M1B in its first official race meeting at St. Jovite, Quebec, but had to retire during practice when the crank broke, causing the Oldsmobile engine to blow up taking the transmission with it. Thus the M1B's official debut was at Mosport in September 1965, with McLaren at the wheel and a whole new engine. It was a successful beginning, with Bruce taking pole and coming a very respectable second as a result of the two heats.

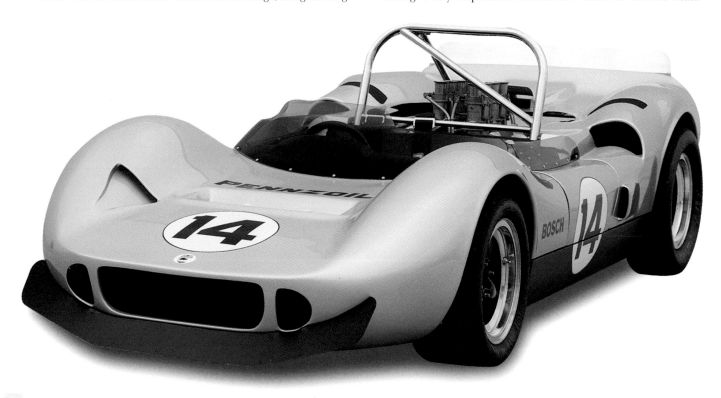

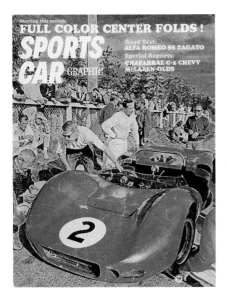

Bruce also ran the M1B in the Los Angeles Times Grand Prix on October 31st, 1965. This time with bigger brakes and tires than before, he was leading the pack until one of his tires began to deflate. The time lost in changing it cost Bruce his leading position and he subsequently finished third.

The first ever Can-Am Challenge Cup series was run in 1966 over six races, four in the United States and two in Canada. The official classification for the Can-Am cars were 'two-seater unrestricted sports cars', meaning they had no upper engine size restriction. All of the races were over about 200 miles and the field would normally consist of about thirty runners. The idea was to complete the series late on in the racing calendar in order that the teams would have fewer conflicting meets. Can-Am became hugely popular with the American public and at many of the participating venues, attendance records were broken. The prize money involved also added to Can-Am's appeal, the total for the season being $358,000, the prize for each race in the region of $30,000. These were not the highest in motor-racing but they were not bad for such a short season.

McLaren continued with the M1B for 1966, but they knew that their 5 litre Oldsmobile engines were not competitive against the heavier but much more powerful 6 litre Chevrolets. These new engines were built of iron, so they weighed an extra 200 lbs but what they lost in weight they certainly made up for in power, supplying an additional 100 bhp. McLaren had no choice but to install the Chevrolet engine, and to harness this new power they fitted a lighter ZF transmission unit, not necessarily because it was the best, but any weight saving was an advantage. In 1966, by adding additional tubes, wider wheels and a separate rear spoiler, McLaren made their 1966 M1B stronger than before. With their new enhanced cars and engines the McLaren drivers (Bruce McLaren and fellow New Zealander Chris Amon) did better in 1966 than ever before.

The first race for the new CanAm cars was at St. Jovite, Quebec

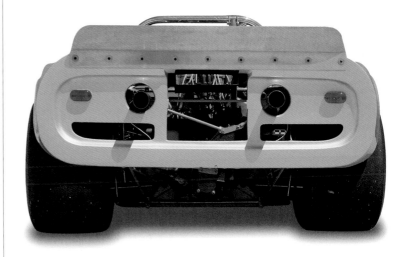

September 11th, and a massive crowd watched an exciting race with Bruce and Amon battling for second and third behind John Surtees in the Lola T70. The second race of this all new series was at Bridgehampton, New York, September 16th and McLaren had their new engines. Amon finished second after another extremely good drive, finishing less than a second behind the leader Dan Gurney. Bruce finished third. Next, to Mosport, where the

15

McLarens were running first and second until Bruce retired after hitting a backmarker and Amon broke his steering; the first Can-Am race with no points for McLaren. The race at Laguna Seca was run over two heats, and neither went particularly well for McLaren, Bruce finished third overall and Amon was nowhere. For the penultimate race of 1966 at Riverside, California, Bruce now had a 5.9 litre fuel injected Chevrolet engine and a body mounted feathering rear spoiler fitted to his M1B which helped him to qualify on his first pole position. However, the engine didn't last long during the race and after about ten laps began misfiring leading to an eventual retirement. Amon started fifth on the grid and retired on the 50th lap with a dead battery. The last race of the highly successful first Can-Am season was at Las Vegas, November 13th, 1966. Amon qualified the faster of the two

McLarens, starting third on the grid, with Bruce fifth. Amon retired with a broken left A-arm but Bruce came through the field and finished the race in second place.

The M1B in the Mathews collection is twelfth of the twenty eight produced. Peter Revson ran this M1B equipped with a Ford engine at the Sports Car supporting race for the British GP at Brands Hatch 1966. It is one of a pair bought by American Bill Kay for himself and Revson to run; unfortunately Kay suffered a fatal heart attack before the GP and his cars were taken over by George Drummond, who took the cars to the Can-Am championship. Later that season, in Nassau for the Bahamas Speed Week and with the Drummond M1B Ford, Revson had a good race leading for most of the way before his brakes failed, but he had completed enough of the circuit to be awarded third. In

Las Vegas for the last race of the 1966 Can-Am series, Revson started ninth on the grid and finished an impressive fourth. In 1967, this M1B was bought by Skip Barber who raced it establishing a new record at Lime Rock. Barber ran the M1B in the first three races of the 1967 Can-Am series. His best starting position was fifteenth at Elkhart Lake on 3rd September and his best finish was seventh in the same race.

Although this chassis has had a long and hard racing life, when the car was acquired early in 2000 for the Mathews Collection it was still in amazingly original condition, and with a little work was brought up to the excellent condition in which it is now seen here.

SPECIFICATIONS

Make: McLaren - Elva	Model: M1-B
Year: 1966	Color: Silver
Engine: Chevrolet V8	CC: 6178
Power: 550 bhp	Transmission: Hewland LG 500
Brakes: Girling Discs	Length: 147"
Width: 59"	Height: 35"
Weight: 1850 lbs	Chassis no: 30-12
Drivers: Peter Revson, Skip Barber	

BOSCH

McLaren-Elva M1C 1967

"Our first McLaren. It gave us the McLaren bug."

The M1C was the last tubular frame chassis car built by Elva as a McLaren customer car. In total, twenty five were built and they were sold in the USA as the McLaren-Elva Mark 3, most of these went on to race in the USRRC and Can-Am championships. The M1C was again based on the space frame design of the M1A and M1B. The M1C was to be the last of the M1s; the McLaren Team had already moved on to the all conquering monocoque M6A.

The M1C was Elva's further development of the M1B with a separate spoiler wing at the rear to replace the airdam. On many

of the American M1Cs this spoiler was adjustable to help with setup at the vastly differing circuits around the States. The M1C chassis was constructed from large diameter round and square tubing in a space frame form with light alloy sheets rivetted and bonded to it, which formed the undertrays and bulkheads. The frame-work was strengthened and stiffened from the M1B by additional tubes in the front and rear bays. The body is formed from four reinforced polyester resin sections with side sections housing the twin 25 gallon rubber fuel cells. The ducting for the brakes, the radiator and oil coolers are all built into the body shape to help with weight saving. The M1Cs were most commonly powered by Chevrolet engines although it was possible to fit the optional Ford or Oldsmobile power units. The whole thing ran on custom made wide McLaren-

Elva cast magnesium wheels, 15 inch diameter at both front and rear.

The M1C in the Mathews collection was originally owned by Jerry Hansen of Minneapolis, USA. He entered it in the 1967 Can-Am series and it had its debut in the first

race of the season at Road America, Elkhart Lake, Wisconsin on September 3rd. The race was also the first time out for Team

McLaren's two M6A's and the initial installment of what was to become known as 'The Bruce and Denny Show'. Thirty two cars started the race, of which seventeen were McLarens, the pair of M6As romped home first and second, while production M1Cs finished 5th, 6th, 7th and 8th. Hansen was placed in the highly respectable 6th position after starting on the seventh row of the grid. He didn't race the M1C again in the 1967 Can-Am series but the one point he got from Road America meant Hansen finished joint 15th in that year's final points standing.

The M1C's ran well throughout all of the 1967 and 1968 seasons and a few raced on for even longer. The most successful M1C driver in 1967 was Chuck Parsons, starting as the first M1C

on every grid that year. Parsons did not, however, fair as well during the races and only managed to get one point for the season from a sixth place at Bridgehampton, New York on September 17th, where his was the only M1C of six to finish the race. At Mosport, Parsons again was the fastest M1C but he had to retire on the 47th lap when his oil pressure dropped. Three of the six M1Cs to start this race made it to the end, the fastest was driven by Skip Scott who finished seventh. At Laguna Seca, four M1Cs started the race but none finished, the last to retire was the forever battling Parsons on the 61st lap with gearbox problems.

Riverside saw an incredible eight M1Cs in the starting line-up although only half of them finished. The difference in performance between these privateers and the factory cars can be seen in the qualifying times. Dan Gurney in his Lola T70 was

fastest here with a lap time of 1:39.3, the quickest M1C was driven by Parsons at 1:44.2, the slowest by Ron Herrera with a time of 1:55.1, which positioned him last on the grid. At Las Vegas, the first M1C casualty was on the first lap when Don Morin crashed, only two M1Cs finished the race, Jerry Entin 7th and Chuck Parsons 10th.

The M1C maintained its popularity into the 1968 Can Am season, with four starting the race at Elkhart Lake. Their form remained the same, with the highest positioning 8th, from a drive by George Eaton. Eaton obviously knew how to get the most out of his M1C and after a 10th at Edmonton on 13th October he drove to an impressive third place at Laguna Seca. His third position was well and truly aided by the torrential rain on race day but it was a tribute to his driving and perseverance that Eaton managed to continue long after the big boys had fallen by the wayside, to get the highest CanAm placing for an M1C. 1969 did not see a decline in the M1Cs popularity and Mosport, for the first race of the season, saw three M1Cs on the grid. John Cordts drove his car to fourth behind Bruce and Denny in their factory McLarens and

John Surtees in a McLaren M12 (the customer version of the M8A). Unbelievably four M1Cs started the 1970 season, still racing competitively three years after their introduction.

This M1C was the Mathews' first ever McLaren. It was such a special car and they had such a good time racing it that it inspired them to start the Mathews McLaren Collection and set them on the road to getting at least one car from each of the series that official Team McLaren cars raced in.

SPECIFICATIONS

Make: McLaren - Elva	Model: M1-C
Year: 1967	Color: Red
Engine: Chevrolet	CC: 6180
Power: 550 bhp	Transmission: Hewland LG
Brakes: Girling Discs	Length: 146"
Width: 66"	Height: 31"
Weight: 1900 lbs	Chassis no: 40-18
Drivers: Jerry Hansen	

McLaren M6A

1967

" Bruce's championship winning car "

This is the original team car that Bruce McLaren drove to the 1967 Can-Am championship.

In April 1967, Robin Herd, an engineer from the aircraft industry, set out to build McLaren's first monocoque Group 7 racer with draughtsman Gordon Coppuck . Using the same monocoque chassis technology as the M5A F1 car, they created the M6A, of which only three were built. The M6A was formed from bonded and rivetted magnesium and aluminum alloy panelling box structures, welded to square section steel tubes. Fuel was carried in three rubber pods, one at either side of the driver and one under his knees. The pods were linked by a series of one-way valves that allowed the fuel to flow around the system under acceleration. The 6 litre engine came from Chevrolet, which, with modification and the addition of fuel injection could produce 525bhp at 7000rpm. The front suspension is formed by outboard coil/damper units with lateral links top and bottom, located by trailing radius rods. In the rear the suspension is upper and lower wishbones with a twin radius rod system. The body is made of fiberglass panelling and the weight is distributed 40 percent front, 60 percent rear. Team McLaren had by now started to produce their own wheels and the M6A ran on 15 inch diameter cast magnesium wheels, 8.5 inch wide at the front and 13.5 inch wide at the back. Team

McLaren had magnificently fulfiled their brief, the car they created was simple and uncomplicated, proving easy to maintain and run.

During the designing stage, special attention was paid to the cars aerodynamics, a pretty new concept at the time. To increase down-force, the M6A was wedge shaped at the front and testing was carried out in a full size wind tunnel to perfect the design. To balance the front end down-force many aerodynamic attachments were tested on the tail, but none seemed to help with the lap times so the only addition was a small molded-in rear spoiler. The most famous and most conspicuous change from any previous McLaren when the M6A debuted was the orange paint work which would go on to become the McLaren trademark color.

Most importantly, the first car, the M6A-1, was ready for testing at Goodwood on June 19th, 1967, more than two and a half months before the start of the season. The car went from paper to prototype in eleven weeks; this led to an on-track development program which enabled the cars to be finally tuned. The plan was to do at least 2,000 practice miles before the start of the season in order to highlight any faults. All the practice and fine tuning paid off and the M6A is one of the finest handling cars and has the best success rate in the history of Can Am.

With the car that is now in the Mathews collection, Bruce McLaren had finally gotten the championship winner he wanted.

a little
something
about
CAN-AM
racing

by
Mark Donohue

Records and landmarks kept falling as the M6A raced past them all; it was the start of the 'Bruce and Denny show'. Bruce McLaren's first ever Can-Am victory was in this car in Laguna Seca, October 15th, 1967. The two McLarens were virtually invincible during 1967 and Team McLaren went on to achieve a total of five victories, three for Denny Hulme and two for Bruce in taking the J-Wax Can-Am championship.

The first race of the season and the M6A's debut was at Road America, Elkhart Lake, September 3rd, 1967. Bruce McLaren qualified in pole position with a time of 2:12.6, beating the lap record which had been set at 2.22.8, meaning he was an incredible ten seconds quicker than any previous entrant in any Formula. Unfortunately Bruce had to retire during the race when his engine ran its bearing. Hulme qualified second but led the race from start to finish, set a fastest race lap, and won by an impressive ninety three second margin.

The McLaren Team's first 1-2 finish came in the next race at Bridgehampton, New York, September 17th. For this event both M6As were fitted with stronger ventilated disc brakes but this was the only change made. Hulme qualified on pole with McLaren second and that's how the race finished. Hulme again led right from the start and even though he spun mid race, no one, not even Bruce, could catch him. The Can-Am series had visited Bridgehampton in

1966 so it is possible to compare race times. The best time in 1966 had been set by Jim Hall in the Chaparral 2E at 1:32.9, Hulme had managed to qualify in 1:29.85, an improvement of just over three seconds.

Just five days after Bridgehampton, McLaren managed to repeat their 1-2 grid starting position in the third race of the season at the Players 200, Mosport Park, September 23rd, 1967. Hulme beat the 1966 qualifying lap record by 2.1 seconds and Jim Clark's Canadian GP time by 1.6 seconds to take pole. Hulme went on to his third consecutive victory, although not without a little drama. By half way through the race, Hulme had a forty second advantage on his nearest contender, Dan Gurney in his AAR T70. During the race, Hulme's steering rack began to work itself loose and two laps from the finish Hulme left the track at Moss Corner, damaging the bodywork which in turn slashed the front left tire. He limped round the last two laps and finished the race creating a thick smoke screen. Bruce finished second, a full half a minute behind Hulme, even though he lost a lap at the start of the race while his team finished fixing a leak in one of his fuel cells, a job which the mechanics hurriedly completed in half the time it normally took. Half way through the season it looked as if Hulme had already done enough to win the Drivers Championship.

The next race was at

Laguna Seca, California, October 15th where Hulme's winning streak seemed to break. He only managed to qualify third after having trouble with his ignition and fuel injection. Bruce got the pole, his first and Team McLaren's consecutive fourth. For the first eight laps the race was led by Dan Gurney in his Lola T70 Mk3b, then his car died and McLaren regained their standard 1-2 position, but this time with Bruce leading Hulme. This is the way the race stayed until the 81st lap of the 106, when Hulme's engine blew. Bruce set the fastest lap time, broke the track record and finished a comfortable first, lapping the nearest contender, Jim Hall in his Chaparral 2G, whose fuel supply was so low he was happy to let Bruce lap him as long as he finished the race. The race was run in extreme heat and all of the drivers felt seriously uncomfortable because of it. Bruce had arranged for one of this team to wait by the circuit wall half way through the race and throw a bucket of water over him!

The penultimate race of the season was the Los Angeles Times GP held at Riverside, California, October 29th. For the first time

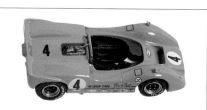

in 1967 there was no McLaren on pole, this accolade was taken by Dan Gurney in his new Gurney-Weslake Ford V8, 0.3 seconds faster than Bruce's M6A in second. Hulme started from third. The race was one of the tightest all season, Gurney led for the first two laps until his engine blew. The front of Hulme's M6A was damaged by a loose tire marker, thrown up by Parnelli Jones' Lola Ford, on the second lap. The damaged bodywork was cut away and Hulme tried to continue the race, only to be black flagged by officials, who believed he had an insufficient amount of the fender left to comply with CanAm rules about bodywork integrity. Bruce finished first, but a mere three seconds ahead of Jim Hall's Chaparral 2G, who had fought him for first the whole race, the two of them swapping the lead on a number of occasions.

The Drivers Championship all depended on the last race, Las Vegas, November 12, 1967. Bruce had thirty points and Hulme had twenty seven, so anything was possible. Hulme only managed a place on the third row after a valve rocker broke during practice but Bruce qualified on pole. The two McLarens were separated by Hall's Chaparral 2G, and the two Lola T70s of Gurney and Jones. Bruce, however, started the race knowing that his engine was mixing oil and water. He had little hope and, sure enough, he had to pull out in the eighth lap. The race was then led by Mark Donohue's Lola until he ran out of fuel. Hulme had a bad start,

SPECIFICATIONS

Make: McLaren	Model: M6-A
Year: 1967	Color: Orange
Engine: Chevrolet V8	CC: 6080
Power: 580 bhp	Transmission: Hewland LG600
Brakes: Discs	Length: 150"
Width: 72"	Height: 38"
Weight: 1733 lbs	Chassis no: 1
Drivers: Bruce McLaren, Mark Donohue	

Bruce McLaren Laguna Seca October 1967

Mark Donohue Watkins Glen July 1968

his belt. Hulme had fought back to third when his usually reliable Chevrolet engine blew up right in from of the grandstand. The winner was John Surtees in his Lola T70, inheriting victory from Mark Donohue's similar T70 that expired half way around the final lap when he ran out of fuel. After five consecutive Team McLaren victories neither car finished in the last race of the 1967 Can Am series, but Bruce McLaren became the second ever Can Am Champion, with Hulme in second place. The competition were nowhere in sight, the nearest contenders in the Drivers Championship were Surtees and Donohue who tied for third, both with sixteen points.

After winning the 1967 Can Am championship, Bruce sold the M6A-1 to Roger Penske for Mark Donohue to run in the 1968 US Road Racing Championship. They installed a 427 ci aluminum Chevrolet engine, painted the car blue as the "Sunoco Special", and in the last year of USRRC racing Donohue became the only driver to win back to back USRRC championships with victories at Laguna Seca, St Jovite, Watkins Glen and Mid Ohio. The car was then sold to Jerry Hansen who continued to race in the Can Am series with little in the way of success, his best result being seventh at Riverside in 1969.

The M6A in the Mathews collection is one of the most historic and important McLaren cars ever. It gave Bruce his first ever Can Am championship and began Team McLarens almost complete domination of Can Am for the next five years. Harry drives his M6A once a year at the Can-Am reunion at Road America.

In 2000, the M6A featured alongside the Mathews M1A at the Goodwood Festival of Speed, the premiere historic and vintage car event of the year anywhere in the world. The Mathews Collection were honored to be invited to take two McLarens to the Goodwood

narrowly missing a huge crash on the first turn but the resulting wreckage could have contributed to a deflating tire which had to be changed. After the pitstop, Hulme began his assent up the field. With Bruce out, all he needed to do was finish fourth to tie on points and the title would be his as he had more victories under

Festival to honor Bruce's achievements before his death on the course, thirty years previous. All the spectators loved seeing the M6A, and for all those involved with the Mathews Collection it was a rewarding experience seeing Harry at the wheel of the M6A driving at a place that was so close to the heart of Bruce McLaren. One of the most significant memories Harry has taken away from the Festival of Speed was driving up the hill and past the Goodwood House in the M6A during the McLaren Parade with Bruce's daughter Amanda in the seat next to him.

Racing was introduced at Goodwood after the Second World War in 1948 by the ninth Duke of Richmond and Gordon. There was nowhere else for motor racing at the time in England, racing on the roads was illegal, Brooklands had been taken over by the aviation industry and Donington was still occupied by the British Army. The perimeter road of the Westhampnett Airfield on the

Duke's estate was turned into the 2.4 mile race circuit. It proved to be an excellent course, really pushing driver skill. It contained double apex curves, a fast straight and challenging corners. The first official race meet was held at Goodwood in September 1948 and it saw the first international race victory for Stirling Moss. Speeds around the course started to increase rapidly and concern was soon expressed over safety. A 3 litre capacity was imposed on all competing cars in 1966 but this was not enough and the circuit closed to all racing events at the end of the year.

The Festival of Speed was started in 1993 by Lord Charles March of Kinrara, the Duke of Richmond's grandson, as a low key affair, to pay homage to the old days of racing at the circuit. It was hoped that 12,000 people may turn up but all estimates were exceeded when in excess of 25,000 arrived to see the mouth watering display. The Festival has continued ever since and is now regarded as the greatest historic racing car event in the world, attracting the most exciting cars and glamourous people. Five years later, Lord March finally achieved his goal of bringing racing back to the old circuit and the Goodwood Revival meeting of 1998 proved a tremendous hit.

McLaren M4B

Following the demise of Group 7 racing in England McLaren decided to build a car for the new 1600cc F2 class. The Robin Herd designed M4A F2 car was announced in February 1967 and was to be built by Lambretta-Trojan. While the M4A was built for Formula 2, the M4B was the Trojan production car for American Formula B racing.

In total, twenty five M4 cars were built in 1967 and 1968. The M4A/B was built from a comparatively simple constant diameter bathtub monocoque, formed from aluminum panelling which was bonded and rivetted to four steel bulkheads. The M4A/B's suspension is double wishbones located by long radius arms front and rear with conventional outboard springs. Fuel is carried in two 10 gallon tanks on either side of the cockpit with a further 5 gallons in a seat back tank. The lower body is formed by the monocoque, the nose and the cockpit surround being fiberglass. The car ran on McLaren Elva cast magnesium wheels, thirteen inch high with seven inch wide rims at the front and ten inch rims

SPECIFICATIONS

Make: McLaren	Model: M4-B
Year: 1967	Color: Orange
Engine: Cosworth FVA	CC: 1600
Power: 240 bhp	Transmission: Hewland FT200
Brakes: Discs	Length: 137"
Width: 70"	Height: 37"
Weight: 960 lbs	Chassis no: 200-27B
Drivers: Chuck Dietrich	

at the rear. The M4B is an extremely light car weighing just over the F2 minimum weight.

One of the M4As was developed for Bruce McLaren to race as an interim Formula 1 car and this was also given the M4B title. McLaren used his M4B between the demise of the M2B and the appearance of the new BRM powered M5. The F1 McLaren M4B was a modified production car, the rear end cut away to hold a BRM 2.1 litre V8 which could give about 280bhp. It also ran with additional fuel tanks prominent on its sides to provide for the GP distance range. Bruce debuted the M4B at the Brands Hatch Race of Champions, were he competed well in Heat 1, but in Heat 2 he missed a gear, over revved and blew up the engine. In total, Bruce drove the F1 M4B in five races with his best finish in the Monaco GP on the 7th May 1967. The M4B's size meant it was exceptional at taking on the winding street circuit course of Monte Carlo, but during the course of the race its battery ran flat and the resulting pit stop for a new one meant he fell from a possible second place to fourth. Bruce went on to crash the M4B at the Dutch GP and then, while testing the repaired car at Goodwood in England, the car caught fire and was totally destroyed.

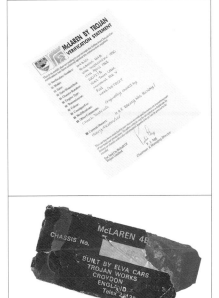

The M4B in the Mathews Collection is one of the Trojan production cars and was originally owned and raced by American Chuck Dietrich. In 1968 Dietrich won 7 races in this car, five in Formula B, and two in SCCA GP Formula Races.

McLaren M6GT

" Bruce's personal roadcar "

The M6GT was a road going development of the McLaren M6 Can Am car. Following the M6's success in Group 7 racing, a proposal was announced to race in the highly lucrative Group 4 GT sports car season for 1969. Group 4 was a highly exciting racing group, with big name teams including Lola, Porsche, Ferrari and Alfa fighting for victory on the European circuits. The plan was to couple the M6 with a closed coupe body for long distance racing. Unfortunately, the homogenisation project hit problems, as new rules were introduced by the FIA for the World Championship of Makes, meaning that a minimum of fifty cars had to be completed before homogenisation was granted. McLaren always intended to sell the M6GT without an engine, leaving that option up to the customer. The project became too big for McLaren to take on and sadly, it was shelved.

McLaren had to forego the racecar but a M6GT was completed for Bruce to test as a prototype for a road car bearing the name 'McLaren'. Bruce had never solely been a driver and his skills as an innovator, designer and motivator had got his company among the ranks of the best in the world. Now that it had sufficient funds, he wanted to get the road car project underway. The plan was to build the highest specification, mid-engined car as possible with safety as an essential feature; to produce two hundred and fifty

units per year of the fastest and quickest accelerating car in the world. McLaren believed they could keep the price down by using a production seven litre Ford engine, this engine would also help to reduce the need for after sales maintenance. Bruce knew that any roadcar McLaren built would be based on the ultimate in racing-derived engineering, and this would be an extremely good way of encouraging sales in the large, lucrative market of the USA.

In total, three or possibly four M6GTs were built but only one of these, OBH 500H, was built at the McLaren racing factory. The other M6GTs were built by Trojan-Lambretta, the company that had the contract to build McLaren's customer cars. One of these was bought by David Prophet who raced it extensively. The car OBH 500H was completed by late 1969 and became Bruce's development car. To put the M6GT through its paces and learn

SPECIFICATIONS

Make: McLaren	Model: M6GT
Year: 1969	Color: Red
Engine: Chevrolet LT1	CC: 5735
Power: 370 bhp	Transmission: ZF type 25
Brakes: Girling Discs	Length: 155"
Width: 68"	Height: 41"
Weight: 1600 lbs	Chassis no: BMR6GT1
Drivers: Bruce McLaren	

what it was truly like as a road car, Bruce adopted it as his personal transportation, and it remained so until he met his untimely death while testing an M8D at Goodwood race track in June 1970. The M6GT had become Bruce's pet project and with his testing and development it would have surely been a great success. Unfortunately, the road car idea died with him and OBH 500H stands as a testament to his vision.

The M6GT was designed by Bruce McLaren and Gordon Coppuck with the help of Jim Clark, Specialist Mouldings' inhouse designer. Specialist Mouldings was the company that produced the fiberglass panels for all the M6s and with his knowledge of the substance, Clark was able to help create a GT body for the M6A chassis. Problems, however, still abounded with the car as it was little more than a race car covered over with a fiberglass body. The

interior space helped to make the M6GT feel a little more like a street car with quilted upholstery and roadcar style instruments. The car was extremely noisy and different sized wheels in the front and rear made carrying a spare an interesting conundrum to solve. The M6GT was also so low that other traffic had problems seeing it. One of the strangest things with the M6GT are the manual

headlights, which, when needed, the driver has to climb out and raise into the upright position by hand, not the ideal on a cold wet British night.

The M6GT, like its Can Am racing forebearers, has a full monocoque chassis with aluminum panelling bonded and rivetted to steel bulkheads. The fuel is held in cells inside the M6GT's two wide pontoons and with its Chevrolet LT1 engine, it had a top speed of 165 mph and could do 0-100 mph in around 8 seconds. Front suspension is with unequal length A-arms, an anti roll bar and Koni dampers, while the rear has trailing arms, an upper link and a lower A-arm with the same anti roll bar and Konis. OBH 500H is separated from the Trojan built M6GTs in that it has its chassis number cast into some of the mechanical pieces including the suspension uprights. The M6GT was fitted with a ZF five speed gearbox, which is a lot lighter than the racing McLaren boxes, making it easier to use on the road. The car is also incredibly light, weighing approximately the same as a Mini, but with a lot more power.

After Bruce's death, Denny Hulme bought his M6GT and

shipped it back to New Zealand for display at the Museum of Transportation and Technology. Hulme was finally persuaded to sell the car in 1990 and it went to a businessman in San Francisco, California. Some time after this, the M6GT was acquired by the Mathews collection.

Apart from its paint the car is entirely original, even having the same tires that Bruce used to surprise people on the quiet English country lanes back in 1969. The M6GT has only been driven a total of just over 1900 miles. Few historic cars have been preserved in such original condition.

" The last of the orange McLarens "

McLaren entered Formula 1 racing on May 22nd, 1966 at the Monaco Grand Prix with Bruce McLaren driving the M2B. The M2B was a monocoque designed by Robin Herd and was powered by a Ford V8 engine with its size reduced from 4.2 litres to the Formula 1 limit of 3 litres. McLaren's first Formula 1 outing was not a success and after starting tenth on the grid, Bruce was forced to retire after nine laps with an oil leak. The engine was the main problem, it was big, heavy and proved to be underpowered and unreliable. It delivered only 300bhp over a very narrow rev band and was unsuited to the GT40 ZF gearbox.

Team McLaren set out to find a new power unit and did so in the shape of Count Volpi's new Serenissima V8, made in Italy to a design by Massimino. The M2B was modified to fit the engine and McLaren went to the Belgium GP at Spa. Again they had no success and the engine ran its bearings on the first lap. The McLaren-Serenissima made its next appearance at Brands Hatch for the British GP. The engine proved reliable and McLaren finished sixth, providing Team McLaren with their first World Championship point. The remainder of the season continued in the same manner and at Mexico in the final GP the engine disintegrated after 40 laps.

Team McLaren had to look elsewhere for engines and they became the first Formula 1 customers for BRM's new four cam V12 engine. The M5A was designed to fit the engine but BRM were not going to be able to deliver on time so Bruce's modified M4B was run in the interim. The M5A was ready for testing in August 1967 and had its race debut at Mosport for the Canadian GP, where after running well, Bruce finished seventh. The M5A was continuously plagued by minor problems and McLaren had another disappointing season.

The 1968 Formula 1 car was the M7A. The new season saw the introduction of the Ford Cosworth DFV engine and with it a change of fortune. The 1967 BRM engine could deliver around 330 bhp, while the new Cosworth DFV produced at least 408 bhp. 1968 also saw Denis Hulme signed to the McLaren Formula 1 team. The M7A was a simple car, its

SPECIFICATIONS

Make: McLaren	Model: M14-A
Year: 1970	Color: Orange
Engine: Cosworth V8 DFV	CC: 3000
Power: 440 bhp	Transmission: Hewland DG 300
Brakes: Lockheed	Length: 156"
Width: 77"	Height: 38"
Weight: 1220 lbs	Chassis no: A3
Drivers: Denny Hulme, Peter Gethin	

monocoque once again designed by Robin Herd. The M7A's debut was in the Brands Hatch Race of Champions with Bruce and Hulme driving. Bruce started from pole and led the race from start to finish, with Hulme coming third. The season did not all go smoothly and by the end it was beginning to look dismal until Hulme won two races and put himself in contention for the Drivers Championship.

The new Formula 1 McLaren for 1969 was the 4 wheel drive M9A. The 4WD meant the car was exceedingly different from any other McLaren, both mechanically and in how it was driven. This caused problems as nobody knew how to utilize the data they were getting from the test drives. The M9A project was short lived, racing only once at the British GP where it suffered an early retirement.

The M14A was the Formula 1 car for 1970. Only three original team M14A's were built. They were designed by Bruce, Gordon Coppuck and Jo Marquart and was a essentially a derivative of the M7 series with several important innovations. The most noticeable change was to mount the rear brakes inboard in an effort to save unsprung weight. Fuel tank size was increased and anti roll bars were tubular to save on weight. The chassis is a full monocoque

with aluminum and magnesium panelling bonded to fabricated steel bulkheads, ending behind the rear cockpit bulkhead. The engine was used as a fully stressed chassis member. The M14A ran on 15 inch McLaren cast magnesium wheels.

The M14A's first race was the South African GP at Kyalami, 7th March 1970. Bruce and Hulme were both driving, with Bruce not finishing, having crashed his car, while Hulme finished an impressive second. The season carried on in this uneven fashion until Bruce's death just before the Belgium GP. The whole team withdrew from the race at Spa, as not only had they lost Bruce but Hulme had badly burnt his hands in an accident at Indianapolis. The team were back for the next race, the Dutch GP at Zandvoort on 21st June, with Dan Gurney taking over from Bruce and Peter Gethin replacing Hulme. Gethin drove his loaned M14/A2 into a

bank, badly crumpling the car. To simplify customs paperwork the team swapped the chassis plates of the A2 and A3 over, meaning that in the German GP on 2nd August, Hulme was not actually driving the original A2. In Germany Hulme drove the 'new' A2 to a third place. He also drove the 'new' A2 at the Austrian, Canadian and United States GP's, retiring in the first two races due to engine failure and managing a seventh in Watkins Glen. 1970 was not a good year for McLaren in Formula 1, not only had they had to suffer the loss of Bruce McLaren, they did not pick up one single championship point. Peter Gethin continued to race the 'new' A2 into the start of the 1971 season. He drove it to an eighth position in the Spanish GP, 18th April, and crashed at Monaco.

The car in the Mathews Collection is the 14/A3 although it has no chassis tag due to it carrying the tag 14/A2 when it was raced. The car is identifiable as the A3 through modifications carried out on its front suspension during the winter period.

McLaren M8D

" First of the big block cars "

On the 2nd June, 1970, Bruce McLaren was killed at Goodwood while testing an M8D, less than two weeks before the beginning of the 1971 Can-Am series. When he died, Bruce was just three months short of his thirty-third birthday and reigning Can-Am champion for the second time in the series, which had been running for just four years. Team McLaren, and indeed motor racing, had lost one of their natural heroes and leaders. The McLaren team responded to Bruce's death by announcing that they would continue by running in the 1970 Can-Am series. They badly needed drivers, so they brought in England's Peter Gethin,

but he would not race initially as Dan Gurney, a good friend of Bruce's, stepped in to help McLaren. After three races Gurney would have to stop competing for McLaren as problems arose with his oil sponsorship contracts clashing with McLaren's Gulf ties. The other team driver was to be Denny Hulme who despite receiving horrendous burns to his hands during an accident at Indianapolis was adamant about leading McLaren to the 1970 Can-Am Championship.

The M8D was a natural evolution of the M8 series. For the 1970 season the FIA introduced rules banning any aerodynamic device above the wheel center line being connected to the suspension. This meant that moving spoilers and wings were banned as were engine intake scoops. As a replacement for the tall wings seen on

the M8B, the M8D has high tail fins with a low wing attached between them. The new aerodynamic features gave the M8D the name 'Batmobile'. Lap times were expected to be slower because of the newly introduced rules, so McLaren concentrated on finding more power. For the first time McLaren had access to the Reynolds Silicon-Aluminum Chevrolet blocks, these new engines had massive capacities. The 8 litre produced 700bhp but for reasons of reliability a 7.6 litre engine was used instead.

Designed by Jo Marquart the M8D was wider, longer and bigger than any Can-Am car before it and 8 inches wider than the M6A with the extra space holding fuel. The monocoque chassis was made from aluminum alloy sheets with a magnesium floor. The transmission forms part of the rear chassis structure.

First race out McLaren proved they were just as effective technically after Bruce's death as before it. Gurney qualified on pole and won at Mosport Park, Ontario, June 14th despite never having seen the M8D before. Hulme drove the other works M8D with his hands still bandaged because of the burns. He qualified second, saving himself for the actual race, which he led from the start. Hulme stayed in front until about half way through the race when he hit a curb and lost some pace. He waved Gurney by, the pain from his hands becoming unbearable and his engine overheating. He eventually finished third, having been lapped twice by Gurney.

Then on to St. Jovite, June 28th, where the starting line up was repeated; Gurney on pole and Hulme second. Gurney led from the start to finish first but Hulme had to retire with an overheated engine. The next race was at Watkins Glen July 12th where Hulme drove with his preferred, but smaller 430 ci engine and Gurney

stuck with a 465 ci. The starting positions were reversed but it was still a McLaren 1-2 on the grid. Hulme's hands had finally healed and it showed in his driving, he led from start to finish. Gurney was in second until his engine began overheating and he dropped back to finish ninth.

Watkins Glen was to be Gurney's last drive of the M8D, Castrol, his oil sponsors, did not like the conflicting interest with the Gulf sponsored McLaren. Gurney had done his job, he had helped the team when they needed him most, keeping McLaren at the top. Peter Gethin was brought in as his replacement. Gethin was the 1969 European F5000 champion, but was no where near as skillful a natural driver as Gurney and even more responsibility was placed on Hulme's shoulders. Gethin had no experience in Group 7 racing and Edmonton, Alberta, July 26th was his debut in the class. He did well, qualifying second to Hulme's pole position and this is how they would finish, Hulme leading Gethin home.

On to Lexington, Ohio, August 23rd and the fifth race of the season. Hulme qualified on pole again, with Gethin pushed back onto the second row. The race was a good one but Hulme still managed to finish over a minute ahead of the rest of the field. Gethin had never been to Lexington before and did not like the course. His engine was also unhappy, and although it was not running at the finish he was awarded ninth. The season was now over halfway through. The sixth of the ten races held at Elkhart Lake, Wisconsin, August 30th. Again the race started with a McLaren on pole and finished with a McLaren 1-2. Hulme had the place at the front of the grid, and Gethin following the senior McLaren driver over the finish. Hulme's victory did not last long, he was disqualified for receiving an alleged push start after his car spun off the track, 13 laps from the end. Gethin's position was upped and he got his first and only Can-Am victory, bringing McLaren's total up to twenty four with nineteen wins in a row. Would their twenty fifth victory come in Road Atlanta, Georgia, September 13th? Things did not start well for McLaren, both drivers were out qualified for pole, having to settle for second and third behind Vic Elford in the Chaparral 2J. The race did not adhere to McLaren's usual formula either. For the first ten laps Hulme led the pack with Gethin second, then he caught up with a group of backmarkers and ran into one, crumpling his cars nose. Hulme limped back to the pits but the impact had bent the chassis and he had to retire. It was now all up to Gethin; he led the race until he hit a patch of oil, lost control and crashed into a bank, causing similar damage to his cars nose as Hulme had done. In the pits the mechanics were able to replace the destroyed nose and Gethin re-entered the race sixth and he was able to regain the lead after all his main competitors had numerous problems with their cars. The glitches, however, did not limit themselves to the opposition and Gethin soon had to retire with gear problems. The McLaren winning streak had ended.

The eighth race of 1970 was held at Donnybrooke, Minnesota. Hulme had a new M8D rebuilt (after his smash at Georgia) from the chassis of the prototype M8E, with an M8B body and suspension. Again neither McLaren managed to qualify on pole, Hulme started second this time behind Revson in the Lola T220

and Gethin fourth, with both drivers suffering mishaps during practice. Hulme only managed to complete a couple of laps before his engine started to play up. He had, however, completed a qualifying lap in 1:30.9, but would it was just slightly too slow to hold of the opposition. Gethin, too, had mechanical problems as his transaxle broke and he got in very few laps. The race was more

successful than qualifying and was a relatively easy race for both drivers. Gethin once again followed Hulme home to resume the norm with a McLaren 1-2. The penultimate race of 1970 was at Laguna Seca, California, October 18th. The McLarens carried on, steamrolling the opposition in qualifying, once again Hulme was first, Gethin second. Gethin spun out of the race on lap forty seven after hitting a patch of oil and running backwards up a bank. The car was unscathed, but stalled and the inboard battery had insufficient power to restart the motor. Victory was left up to Hulme, who had a battle on his hands with Jackie Oliver in his 'Titanium Car', Lola T122 MkII. He won the race but only by of 1.2 seconds, the smallest margin that competitors or crowds had seen for a long time.

The 1970 Can-Am season finished in Riverside, California, November 1st. Again no pole for McLaren, Hulme beaten back to second once again by Elford in the Chaparral and Gethin way down in sixth. Hulme led fairly comfortably from start to finish but Gethin did not make it to the flag, on the twenty first lap his engine blew up and with it went his hopes of a second place in the Drivers Championship. Hulme won the Drivers Championship with 132 points and a 67 point cushion from the rest of the pack and although Gethin missed out in second place it still went to a McLaren mounted driver, Lother Motschenbacher in his M8C. McLaren had won 8 out of the 10 Can-Am races in 1970 and with it the Championship. The M8D was a truly successful car.

The story behind the M8D in the Mathews collection is very

The car was first raced as a Gardos McLaren at the Wanneroo race circuit in Perth in 1972. It was campaigned throughout Australia by O'Sullivan and later by Keith Poole until it went to the USA in 1991.

In 2000, the Mathews M8D raced in the feature Can-Am race at Elkhart Lake, where Greg Mathews set the fastest lap time of 2:09.347. In 1970 at the Elkhart race, Hulme in the M8D qualified at 2:10.6 and had the fastest lap at 2:12.4. A comparison of these two results shows just how well the Mathews cars are kept, in order that they can still run as fast and well as they did in their heyday.

unusual and a bit difficult to trace. The car was shipped in parts to Australia in 1971 and was assembled there to avoid high duty imposed on complete cars. The car was assembled by James Gard, Don O'Sullivan's engineer, from drawings supplied by McLaren.

McLaren M19C

The M14 series of Formula 1 cars, of which there is a fine example in the Mathews Collection, did not prove to be as successful as people had hoped, so, for the 1971 Formula 1 season, McLaren set about designing an entirely new car.

The M19 was designed by Ralph Bellamy, who came to McLaren from Brabham. He was brought in as Gordon Coppuck, McLaren's usual designer, was committed to working on the Can-Am and Indianapolis projects. Bellamy's new car, the M19A, had its press premiere in February 1971 and had a distinctive 'coke bottle' shape, wider and longer than any McLaren F1 car before it. The swollen shape around the cockpit was to hold the majority of the fuel around the center of the wheelbase to improve road holding. The M19A had a tall airscoop placed on the Cosworth DFV engine and a center pillar mounted rear wing, but the greatest change was in the suspension. Rising rate suspension was devised with front and rear inboard coil springs/damper units. The effect of this was that the springs compressed as the suspension deflated, meaning the faster the car was going, the harder the suspension became.

The M19A had an aluminum monocoque with a 100 inch wheelbase, an increase of 5 inches on the M14. The increase in length allowed more fuel to be stored in the space between the driver and the engine at the rear of the tub. The body was formed from fiberglass panels made once again by Specialised Mouldings. The inner skin was formed from NS4 aluminum alloy sheeting which was shaped over internal bulkheads, the outer layer was created from regulation thickness sheets intended to stop impact penetration.

Initial practice with the M19A-1 looked encouraging and it was taken to Kyalami, South Africa for the first race of the 1971

SPECIFICATIONS

Make: McLaren	Model: M19C
Year: 1972	Color: White
Engine: Cosworth Ford DFV V8	CC: 3000
Power: 430 bhp	Transmission: Hewland DG300
Brakes: Lockheed	Length: 178"
Width: 86"	Height: 44"
Weight: 1230 lbs	Chassis no: M19C-2
Drivers: Denny Hulme, Peter Revson	

Formula 1 series. Hulme drove the M19A-1 and Peter Gethin partnered him in the M14A. The race at Kyalami was incredibly exciting, Hulme led from the start, battling almost all the way to keep Andretti's Ferrari from taking the lead. Then, just four laps from the finish, Hulme's rear suspension broke, causing it to steer and his position slipped from first to sixth at the flag; this was the best result the M19A-1 attained. One of the problems with it was the suspension; the stumbling block was a lack of knowledge about what happened to the driving when the suspension was working correctly. For example, the cars suffered from massive vibrations that the McLaren team could not fix. The cause was the suspension working at its optimum, but this was not realized at the time. After much testing, it was discovered that the rising rate suspension was of no advantage at the rear and so they reverted to conventional suspension.

The M19As with standard rear suspension continued to be run into the first part of 1972 alongside the M19C as it was introduced. The M19C differed little from the M19A, it was lighter but the largest and most obvious difference to appear on the M19C was new paint. In 1972 the McLaren orange gave way to Yardley Cosmetics sponsorship and their livery, while Goodyear and Gulf kept their places as co-sponsors. Peter Revson was signed by McLaren to partner Hulme in the 1972 Formula 1 season. They also enlisted two other drivers who they believed would help them to victory, Brian Redman and Jody Scheckter.

The first race of the 1972 Formula 1 season was held in Argentina on 23rd January. Both Hulme and Revson drove M19As, starting third and fourth consecutively on the grid behind Carlos Reutemann in the Brabham BT-34 on pole and Jackie Stewart, in a Tyrrell 003, in second. Stewart went on to win the race, beating Hulme into second by an impressive twenty-six second gap. Revson had to retire on the fiftieth lap after spinning his M19A. McLaren ran the two M19As again at Kyalami, South Africa, 4th March. Jackie Stewart's Tyrrell 003 qualified on pole, and the McLarens were knocked right back down the field, Hulme starting fifth and Revson

his first front row starting position, although Jacky Ickx in a Ferrari 312B2 got the all important pole. Revson again started far down the pack in eleventh. Hulme led the race for the first four laps before Stewart's Tyrrell overtook him. Hulme had to retire on the forty eighth lap when his gearbox pinion bearing broke. Revson drove a steady race and finished fifth. Fittipaldi in the all conquering JPS Lotus 72D once again won the race.

The M19C finally appeared in round 4, the Monaco GP on 14th May, driven by Hulme. Revson had commitments at Indianapolis so Brian Redman drove the M19A. Pole position went to Fittipaldi in the

twelfth. Hulme had driven the M19A well in Kyalami in 1971 and this time his impressive driving skills were obvious again, his luck held and he won the race. Revson came in third, twenty-five seconds behind Hulme. The two McLaren drivers were separated by Emerson Fittipaldi's JPS Lotus 72D, the driver who had beaten Hulme to first place in the 1971 event.

At Jarama on 1st May for the Spanish GP, McLaren were still running the two M19As driven by Hulme and Revson. Hulme got

Lotus, the best McLaren could muster was seventh for Hulme and tenth for Redman. Both McLarens finished the race, quite a task on Monte Carlo's twisting tiny streets, Redman fifth and Hulme fifteenth. Revson was back for the Belgium GP at Nivelles Baulers on 4th June 1972, driving the M19A with Hulme in the M19C. Hulme began the race third on the grid, once again ahead of his team mate's seventh and they finished the race in these positions. The French GP was no better with the same mediocre results,

Hulme's M19C seventh and Redman in the M19A was ninth. The British and German GPs had McLaren continuing with Revson or Redman in the M19A and Hulme in the M19C, and it was not until Osterreichring, Austria, 13th August that there were two M19Cs on the grid. McLaren had their best result all season, Hulme only one second behind the victorious Fittipaldi, Revson third. Hulme also claimed the fastest lap time of 134.485 mph on lap 47. Italy, 10th September, was next and still no win, Hulme came home third, Revson just less than

twelve seconds behind him in fourth. McLaren had to wait for the penultimate race of the year at Mosport Park, Canada on 24th September for a pole position; Revson achieved this with a lap time of 1:30.60, Hulme started in second. Neither McLaren ever got to lead the race, they were both beaten into the first corner by Peterson in a March 721G, but he lost the lead to Stewart's Tyrrell 005 on the third lap. Stewart remained in the lead and finished first, Revson came second and Hulme third. The last Grand Prix race of 1972 was held at Watkins Glen, USA on 8th October 1972. Three McLarens started, the additional car was an M19A driven by young

South African driver, Jody Scheckter. Hulme came third, Scheckter ninth and Revson retired on the fifty fourth lap with ignition failure. McLaren had gone a whole year with only one win; the whole season was virtually sewn up by Fittipaldi's Lotus and Stewart's Tyrrell. McLaren came third in the Constructors Championships, and in the Drivers Championship, Hulme came third and Revson fifth.

The M19C was effectively made illegal in 1973 by the introduction of deformable structural regulations. However, these regulations did not come into force until the fourth round and the Spanish GP, so the M19C was run at Argentina, Brazil and South Africa, all with minimal success. McLaren then introduced the M23 and they finally had a winning car in Formula 1 again.

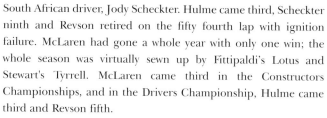

McLaren M8E

The M8E was the Trojan production car for the 1971 season, the M8F designation went to the Team McLaren works cars. The M8E body shape was based on a combination of the M8B and M8D. The M8E has a 4 inch narrower track, with a smaller more robust fiberglass body than the M8D and instead of the side fins, it had a low strut supported rear wing, making a weight saving of 22lbs. The prototype M8E was tested briefly by Denny Hulme at Goodwood in 1970 before the batch of customer cars were built.

The M8E that is now in the Mathews Collection, was originally delivered to Roy Woods Racing for Vic Elford to drive. The first race of the season was, as always, at Mosport on 13th June but Elford's car was not ready for this race. The only M8E to enter was driven by Roger McCaig; he started sixth on the grid and drove well, finishing tenth. Cars with the McLaren name took the first five places, with the works drivers coming first and second in their brand new M8Fs. For St Jovite, Quebec on June 27th, McCaig was once again the only M8E but he did not fair as well as at Mosport, retiring on the thirty third lap with damaged body work.

Vic Elford was an old hand at Can-Am and had driven five different cars in the 1970 season, a Porsche 917, an AVS Shadow, Lola T70 Mk 3B, McLaren M6B and most importantly the Chaparral 2J. The Chaparral was a revolution in racecar design, dubbed the 'sucker car', which used a system of fans and a series of skirts around the lower body edge to help stick it to the road. Elford drove the Chaparral twice, at Road Atlanta and at Riverside, both times qualifying on pole and over one second faster than the rest of the opposition. What the Chaparral gained in technology it lost in reliability, at Road Atlanta he finished a very respectable sixth but at Riverside Elford had to retire on the fifth lap with engine failure. Roy Wood Racing finally had their M8E ready for July 11th and the meet at Road Atlanta, Georgia. Elford swapped his Chaparral for the hopefully more reliable M8E and qualified on the fifth row, six positions ahead of the only other M8E, once again driven by McCaig. Elford's race did not go to plan and was classified 17th after he retired on lap thirty five with clutch failure. McCaig in his M8E fared better, finishing the race in seventh.

SPECIFICATIONS

Make: McLaren	Model: M8-E Can Am
Year: 1971	Color: Yellow
Engine: Alloy Chevrolet	CC: 8095
Power: 700 bhp	Transmission: Hewland LG-500
Brakes: Lockheed Discs	Length: 153"
Width: 74"	Height: 36"
Weight: 1800 lbs	Chassis no: 80-04
Drivers: Vic Elford, Sam Posey	

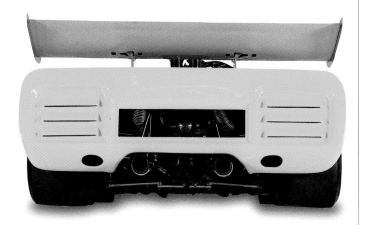

Elford and McCaig were again the only two M8Es on the grid at Watkins Glen, 25th July. The race was filled with cars and drivers from the 6 hour endurance race that had been run on the track the previous day. The fastest of these contenders was Mark Donohue in the Penske Ferrari 512M, the quickest of the usual participants was unusually not one of the team McLaren drivers but Jackie Stewart in the Lola T260. Elford and McCaig qualified 14th and 21st respectively; Elford finished a well contended 8th while McCaig retired early on in the race with suspension failure. At Lexington, Ohio on 22nd August was the fifth race of 1971, and this time four M8Es began the race. Elford and McCaig were joined by Bob Brown and George Drolsom. None of them finished the race but they were in good company as neither did the McLaren works drivers, both going out after suffering from U-

Joint cross failure. Denny Hulme's U-Joint went on the first corner, causing him to spin in front of the oncoming pack, and in the confusion that ensued as drivers tried to avoid the disabled McLaren, any order in the way the drivers started was scratched as McCaig moved up to fourth from his grid position of fourteenth. McCaig drove well for the entirety of the race and once again was the highest ranking of the M8Es, classified thirteenth even though his engine blew on lap 64. Drolsom retired on the fifty sixth lap with mechanical failure, Elford on the twenty seventh lap, suffering from heat exhaustion and Brown only lasted eleven laps before his car caught fire.

The season was now into its second half and Hulme and Revson, the two McLaren works drivers, were again running away with the Championship. For the first time all year, at Road America, Elkhart Lake, Wisconsin on August 29th, McCaig did not run his M8E, and Elford and Brown were the only two drivers with the car. Elford had his best start in the M8E with a position on the third row, Brown was only three places behind in tenth. Drolsom was driving, but he had reverted to a M8C after the race at Mid-Ohio. In the race, Brown was a non starter but Elford finished the highest yet for an M8E in a superb third behind Revson and Jo Siffert in a Porsche 917. Donnybrooke was to be Elford's last race in the M8E. He continued his prosperous streak with a position on the third row of the grid. Three other M8Es were driven by Brown, McCaig and Fred Parkhill. It was a good race for

the M8Es, with three of the four starters finishing the race. Elford once again showed the immense amount of driving skill that had got him the drive in the Chaparral, finishing fourth behind three other McLarens; the two works drivers, and Greg Young in a modified car classed as an M8E/D. Brown finished eighth and Parkhill fifteenth. McCaig retired on the thirty first lap with a broken rim.

In Edmonton, Alberta September 26th there were only two M8Es, one driven by the ever present McCaig, the other by Brown. The weather was appallingly wet and all the drivers struggled, with both the qualifying and race times down on previous years. Brown started in tenth, McCaig in, unlucky for some, thirteenth place. Both M8E drivers fell foul of the weather, McCaig on the first lap, Brown on the twenty ninth.

In pre-race testing at Laguna Seca, California on October 17th, Elford returned with the Roy Woods M8E and the reason they had missed Edmonton now became apparent; it now had ex-works M8D body panelling on the narrow M8E tracks. Elford crashed the M8E/D backwards into a bridge abutment at around 100mph. Luckily he walked away from the crash but the chassis was a complete wreck. Elford competed in the race, driving a M8D with

a M8E tub, and although he found this a far more satisfactory way to combine the cars, he retired from the race on sixty eighth lap when his engine died and he could not restart it.

The Roy Woods team rebuilt the M8E around a new tub for the Los Angeles Times GP at the Riverside for the tenth and last race of the season. Sam Posey drove it well and qualified fourth on the grid. He finished in fourth position, one lap behind the victorious Hulme. McCaig was the only other M8E driver, starting thirteenth and finishing seventh. The car was then sold to Alan Johnson of SCCA fame who debuted at Mid Ohio, August 6th, 1972 where he finished 13th. After passing through several further owners the Mathews Collection acquired this well used car and returned it to its original specification and Elford livery.

"Last of the McLaren Can-Am championship winners "

P eter Revson, driving the factory, M8F won the 1971 Can-Am championship and in doing so became the first American to win the title. The M8F was the last all conquering Can-Am McLaren, in total McLaren won eight of the ten races of the 1971 season, an impressive feat but it would be their last year of absolute dominance.

The McLaren M8F was designed by Gordon Coppuck, who created the strongest, longest, widest, biggest and heaviest McLaren ever. The M8F chassis was a monocoque with steel bulkheads and a heavier gauge Reynolds aluminum inner and outer skins than previously, making it more robust. Fuel was stored in the monocoque at either side of the driver in four foam filled rubber cells with a complete capacity of 72 US gallons. The additional size and weight improved the handling and braking of the car and made it possible for the rear brakes to be moved inboard. Track dimensions were slightly narrower to allow the 17" wide rear rims to fit within the same overall body width. Body shape had actually changed very little from the other M8s, and was a natural evolution from the M8D "Batmobile" shape.

Aerodynamic fences were fitted all along the tops of the body sides, which rose up into tail fins to act as a mount for the broad rear wing. The nose was also re-shaped. The improvements in aerodynamics and the addition of the wing created a massive 1.5 tons of downforce. It is like all McLarens, an uncompromised race car built only for winning.

Revson joined Team McLaren in 1971 to race alongside Denny Hulme in the sixth Can-Am series. The first race, as always, was at Mosport, Ontario on June 13th. In pre-race preparations the McLaren proved that once again they outclassed almost all of the opposition although their engines were slightly less easy to drive as in previous years. Hulme qualified second, Revson third, the fly in McLaren's ointment was Jackie Stewart's Lola on pole. Hulme started the race like a true reigning champion, putting five seconds between himself and all the other cars within five laps. McLaren got an easy 1-2 with Hulme leading Revson home.

So on to St. Jovite, Quebec, June 27th, were Hulme qualified on pole. Revson had been driving in the USAC Pocono event and had little time to perfect his M8F for the circuit, so he was fortunate to start third. The car dividing the

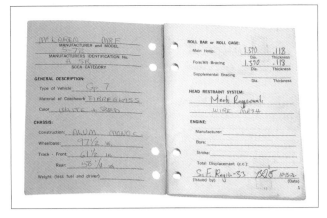

McLarens was once again Stewart's Lola and he drove to victory, beating an ill Hulme into second. McLaren were not used to being beaten and so went to Road Atlanta, Georgia early for some additional practice. On July 11th Revson started the race with a all aluminum Reynolds 479 cubic inch engine for the first time in the season. Hulme had problems with his regular Chevrolet engine, two breaking during practice, but even with these problems McLaren once again got their almost standard 1-2 starting position. The two McLaren's got away in front, with Revson leading Hulme and this is the way they finished. Hulme, whose brakes had not been right for the entire race, finished 20 seconds behind Revson.

At Watkins Glen on July 25th, McLaren were again beaten off pole by the Lola. Revson again raced with a Reynolds sleeveless block but this one was enlarged with a longer throw crank to bring the displacement up to 509 ci. Stewart, in the Lola, got off first with Revson second, Hulme third and this was the way it stayed until the tenth lap when Stewart had to make a pit stop for a flat tire. Stewart was battling back when his car started vibrating strongly and he retired and with him went any opposition McLaren would feel in the race and they coasted home, Revson first.

When the Can-Am circus turned up to race at Mid-Ohio, Lexington, August 22nd they found it was in a bad state of repair. The surface was bad, but the amount of trees and poles positioned around the course were too dangerous and the night before the race trees were cut down and banks built to make the drive

relatively safe. During practice, both McLarens and the Lola had problems caused by the road surface, Revson's M8F bending many suspension members at its rear. The McLaren cars occupied the front row of the grid and Hulme beat Revson into the first corner where he spun right in the way of the oncoming pack. With one exception everyone managed at get past safely but any order of the cars in the group were ruined. Revson and Stewart had survived the foray and the McLaren was leading the Lola. Stewart had decided that he could not race his car competitively as it would simply not last, so he sat back, allowing the gap between himself and Revson to grow on every lap. It looked as if the race was a foregone conclusion from that point on, until the 77th lap when the outer U-joint on Revson's M8F broke exactly as it had done on Hulme's, the cause of his crash. Stewart's tactics had paid off and for the second time in the season he beat the two McLarens.

A Simple McLaren M8-F

The 1971 Can-Am season was now past its halfway point with the sixth race held at Elkhart Lake, Wisconsin on 29th August. Both McLaren drivers spent the first day of qualifying in California practising for a USAC race. Hulme returned early after engine problems forced him to retire from that event and after a few laps back at Can-Am, qualified fastest. Revson stayed at the USAC event to get a place on the front row there, knowing this would mean starting from the back of the grid at Elkhart Lake. Revson

McLaren M8F

SPECIFICATIONS

Make: McLaren	Model: M8-FP
Year: 1972	Color: Orange
Engine: Alloy Chevrolet V8	CC: 8360
Power: 850 bhp	Transmission: Hewland LG600 Mk.II
Brakes: Lockheed Discs	Length: 167"
Width: 78"	Height: 44"
Weight: 1850 lbs	Chassis no: M8F5-72
Drivers: Warren Agor	

drove an exceptional race, fighting his way up through the other drivers and by the seventh lap he was fourth and by the eighth lap, third. When Stewart's Lola started puffing out smoke on the tenth lap, Revson inherited second. Hulme in the meantime was well in the lead with no competition and the McLaren's were settling back for another 1-2. Then suddenly Hulme stopped with a broken crankshaft, and Revson went onto a very unexpected victory.

Donnybrooke, Minnesota September 12th, was another typical McLaren race with a Revson-Hulme front row. Revson comfortably led the entire race while Hulme battled against the Lola for a third of the race until he stopped for an impromptu pitstop and Hulme went through into second. The race on September 1971 at Edmonton, Alberta was almost another story. Once again the starting grid had a McLaren front row but when it came to starting the engines, mechanics heard a sickening noise come from Revson's M8F. On investigation, a 3/8th inch bolt was found in one of the McLaren cylinder heads, but by the time it was removed and the engine rebuilt, Revson was down by

eleven laps. Stewart's Lola had had an aerodynamic redesign, the front end was stubbier with fencing and a overhanging wing and this, combined with rain, allowed the Lola to pull away and lead for nearly the whole race. Stewart had a comfortable lead until about half way through the race and then Hulme starting pulling back his lost time. Stewart made a small mistake and ended up on the grass, when he returned to the tarmac, the Lola was not responding properly and Hulme was gaining even faster. Thirteen laps from the end, Stewart spun the Lola and Hulme took first place, his first Can-Am victory in three months. Revson did not manage to repeat his comeback of Elkhart Lake and he finished twelfth.

The penultimate race was held at Laguna Seca, California on October 17th and Revson qualified again on pole with a record

breaking lap, knocking just 0.02 seconds off of the previous record. Hulme qualified second and in this formation, with the ever fighting Stewart in third, they started the race. After ten laps Hulme's engine refused to pull over 6000 rpm and he dropped back, by then there was no way Stewart could catch Revson who had a 25 second lead. That is until Revson struck a backmarker, which almost ripped off the right door and meant a 12 second pitstop to fix it; Stewart was now within fighting range but he could not close the gap. Twenty laps from the end Revson's engine began to loose power and with just two laps to go smoke started coming out of the M8F's right exhaust pipe. On his last lap Revson was black flagged because of the smoke and for dropping oil but he ignored it and drove on to finish the race first, but it was Stewart who got the checkered flag. A mass debate ensued but in the end the race went to Revson with a fine of $250.

The last race of the 1971 Can-Am series was held at Riverside, California October 31st, and the drivers championship was still undecided between Hulme and Revson. Both McLarens had sleeveless 509 ci engines and Hulme qualified on pole determinately beating the circuit's previous lap record; Revson simply could not match his speed and qualified second. Hulme raced into the first corner and away while Revson held off Stewart's Lola. Hulme never looked back, he did not push the car too hard but carried on increasing his lead. Revson didn't need to win, just to do better than sixth and by doing so he became the first ever American Can-Am champion. Revson had won five races and had 142 points, Hulme three victories but was not far behind with 132 points.

In 1972 Trojan built the M8FP, the production car of McLaren's previous years team car the M8F. The M8FP in the Mathews Collection was originally owned and raced by Warren Agor.

McLaren M20

" Last of the all conquering McLaren Can-Am cars "

This M20 is the factory team car that Denny Hulme drove in the 1972 Can-Am Championships. It is the car that he won his last Can-Am race in at Watkins Glen, New York.

1971 was the last time that McLaren won the Can-Am Championship and 1972 was the last year that they entered a factory team. Porsche's technological advances had been so great that McLaren could no longer compete with them or the Porsche budget. McLaren had never been the most innovative team but their cars had always been reliable, they lost this reliability in 1972 and this added to the extent of their demise. When they retired at the end of 1972 McLaren held a record breaking 43 victories including a staggering 19 consecutive race wins between 1968 and 1970.

The M20 was a new beginning after the M8 series had reached its natural conclusion. It was designed by Gordon Coppuck who's idea was to create another Can-Am winner but in a different form, with the weight concentrated within the wheelbase. Coppuck also want to insulate the drivers from the radiator to make their job easier. The most radical thing that Coppuck did was for the first time use an under-seat fuel tank which ran the entire length of the cockpit directly behind the drivers back, which in conjunction with the two side mounted cells held a total of 79 gallons of fuel. This method of storing the fuel in the outer section of the monocoque ensured a low center of gravity and gave the car its distinctive "Coke bottle" shape. Another change was side mounting the radiators, at the drivers hip and behind the cockpit, instead of having it situated in the nose, this allowed a wing to be mounted on the nose. This full length fully adjustable wing was mounted between the front fenders and when combined with the strut mounted rear wing improved down-thrust, traction and cornering. The M20 was built with the intention of running it with a turbocharged engine but the engine could not be organized in time so McLaren started the season with a Chevrolet engine. The 8.1 litre engine was a stressed unit part of the chassis. It was constructed from 16 and 20 gauge L72 aluminum alloy with Argon welded steel bulkheads. The suspension pick up points are taken from the steel bulkheads to give maximum strength. Only three were built.

Preparation for the 1972 season started well and on November 2nd 1971 McLaren announced that Jackie Stewart was signed up to partner Denny Hulme as the McLaren team drivers. During pre-season practice at Silverstone both drives clocked up record breaking lap times and McLaren believed they were on the way to another victorious season. Then just days before the start of the season Stewart was taken ill with a duodenal ulcer and on doctors

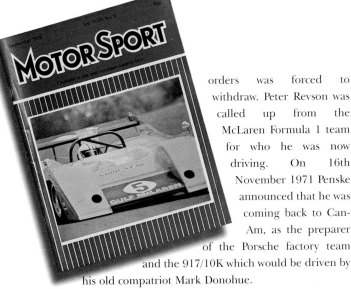

orders was forced to withdraw. Peter Revson was called up from the McLaren Formula 1 team for who he was now driving. On 16th November 1971 Penske announced that he was coming back to Can-Am, as the preparer of the Porsche factory team and the 917/10K which would be driven by his old compatriot Mark Donohue.

The 1972 season started at Mosport Park, June 11th, and the 50th ever Can-Am race. On the starting grid Revson was second, Hulme third and ominously Donohue's brand new Porsche was on pole. Revson slightly jumped the flag at the beginning of the race proper but by the first corner Donohue's Porsche was in the lead. What nobody at McLaren knew was that more power in the Porsche had taken away from its reliability and the Porsche led the race until it had induction system problems and had to stop for an impromptu pitstop, when he returned he was three laps behind the leaders. Revson inherited the lead and managed to hold onto it until two laps from the end when disastrously his engine blew. Hulme took the lead and the race but the signs were not good, Donohue had fought back from ninth to third and narrowed the gap between him and the other drivers by an incredible amount.

At Road Atlanta McLaren's M20 had improved aerodynamics, brakes and tires and were all round better than at Mosport. Things did not fair well though with Revson having a massive engine blow up in practice. Hulme's M20 was running well and his McLaren and the Porsche, this time driven by George Follmer, were almost neck-and-neck with Hulme just scraping pole, with Revson on second. The first three laps were tight, the Porsche just leading the two McLarens. On the third lap Revson's magneto rotor broke and he pulled over to fix it. When Hulme reached where Revson was on the next lap, Revson saw his team mate's M20 rear up and do a 180mph back flip, the car was totally destroyed and Hulme luckily completely recovered after a short time in hospital.

In just nine days the prototype M20 was built up to race quality

SPECIFICATIONS

Make: McLaren	Model: M-20
Year: 1972	Color: Orange
Engine: Alloy Chevrolet	CC: 8095
Power: 750 bhp	Transmission: 5 Speed Hewland
Brakes: Discs	Length: 181"
Width: 81"	Height: 46"
Weight: 1900 lbs	Chassis no: M20-003
Drivers: Denny Hulme	

for Hulme at Watkins Glen. The McLarens were running well and extremely fast, Revson qualified on pole and Hulme second. They finished 1-2 but with the order reversed, Hulme got ahead of Revson on the first corner and stayed there leading the first McLaren double victory of 1972 and his twenty second.

At Mid Ohio Hulme finished fourth while Revson failed to finish. Road America showed a very brief return to form, with Hulme comfortably qualifying for pole and leading the race until ignition failure put him out after just 12 laps. Things were getting

worse for McLaren and at Donnybrooke again both drivers had to retire after a short but promising start. Edmonton was a little better for McLaren, Hulme leading for 31 laps and finishing second, and Revson finished 6th. At least the McLarens completed the race but Porsche were still winning. Both McLarens retired at Laguna Seca and George Follmer and the Penske Porsche took the title, in the same all encompassing fashion McLaren had done five years previous. The final race of the season, the Los Angeles Times GP started looking as if there would be a race between the Porsches and the McLarens. It did not last long and Hulme eventually retired although Revson did go on to take second in the last appearance of Team McLaren in the Can Am series. Hulme was runner up in the Championship points with 65 compared to Follmer's 130. Revson was sixth with 48. McLaren would no longer enter the Can Am series, as they could not compete with the money Porsche had invested in Turbo technology.

The M20 in the Mathews collection was originally the McLaren team works prototype M20, but after Hulme wrote off his M20/2 at Road Atlanta the M20/3 was called into service as his team car. The Mathews car made its debut at Watkins Glen, New York on

July 23rd where Hulme drove it home to his last ever Can-Am win. The M20/3 was Hulme's car for the rest of the season when he finished second in the drivers championship.

At the end of the 1972 season the M20/3 was bought by Felder Racing Team from Team McLaren's Teddy Mayer. Felder Racing ran the car at the Interserie in 1973, during which time they fitted a turbocharged engine but had little success. In 1974 they reverted to the fuel injected Chevrolet 494 engine and finished second overall in the Interserie, just one point off a tie for first place. In 1979 the M20/3 was bought by Skip Berg, the owner of Sears Point Raceway, and he restored the car to its 1972 Can-Am trim. The car in the Mathews collection is one of only two M20's that can claim original tubs. The M20/3 still has its original chassis, suspension and most of its original running gear down to the same valve covers the car had in 1972.

67

McLaren M22

" The unknown and unloved McLaren "

The McLaren M22 is almost a 'forgotten' McLaren and there is little known about it.

British F5000 was born in 1967 from the need for a crowd drawing, financially viable, single seat formula. At the same time, The Sports Car Club of America decided that they wanted to attract more attention to their single seater races, so they modified their Formula A to allow admissions by cars powered by stock block 5 litre engines. Interest in both events was aroused and F5000 was born in the UK, with cars limited to a 5000cc maximum capacity and 500 bhp.

McLaren's first F5000 was designed by Gordon Coppuck and based on the M7A Formula 1 car. The most substantial changes that Coppuck made were additions at the rear of the tub to accommodate the Chevrolet 5 litre V8 engine. The new car was named the M10A and was built by Trojan, with almost all of the seventeen car production run aimed for America and its lucrative market. Only one M10A stayed in the UK and was raced by Peter Gethin. It was actually the prototype McLaren built chassis which Bruce McLaren himself had tested and was a high performing car, the one to beat. Gethin went on to win the Guards 5000 Championship that year. The M10A had been so successful that

SPECIFICATIONS

Make: McLaren	Model: M-22
Year: 1972	Color: Orange
Engine: Chevrolet	CC: 4950
Power: 500 bhp	Transmission: Hewland DG5
Brakes: Discs	Length: 176"
Width: 77"	Height: 50"
Weight: 1450 lbs	Chassis no: 3-72
Drivers: Harry Engle	

Trojan went on to build twenty-one M10Bs. The M10B was a mild improvement on its predecessor with, among other changes and weight saving initiatives, an engine that was lowered by 2 inches. The M10B continued the McLaren cars winning streak at F5000, winning the European F5000 championship, and it was a highly popular customer car.

In 1972 McLaren replaced the M10B with the stressed engine M18 but it proved to be a mistake. The M18 was difficult to set up and was unpredictable when cornering. Brian Redman, a highly talented driver, ran the works M18 during its first season, but only managed two victories from the sixteen starts he made.

David Hobbs, a British driver who had found victory in America with a M10B, was recruited late in 1971 to test a modified M18. McLaren's F5000 cars had also found fortune at the Tasman Championships in Australasia and it was in this series that Hobbs drove the prototype M18/22 at Pukekohe for Round 1 of the Tasman Championship on the 8th January 1972. In the

supposedly Formula 1 series, all but four of the starters were F5000 cars and Hobbs qualified seventh on the grid. He drove a determined race and took third on the 48th lap, and this is the position in which he finished the race, 4.1 seconds behind the winner, Frank Gardner, in his Lola T300 Chevrolet. Unfortunately the new car had the same M18 tendencies and it was not until the final race of the season that Hobbs had it sorted out enough to win; by this time, McLaren works were preparing the new production car, named the M22, for the European F5000 series. The major problem with the whole concept of the car was that the McLaren works had lost a lot of interest in the F5000 series and instead were concentrating on the more glamourous Can-Am, Indy and Formula 1 series. Without the support and back up of the works, Trojan stopped making F5000 cars late in 1972.

Belgian Teddy Pilette was hired to drive a M22 for VDS racing but delivery was late and in the interim they had to race the well used M18/22. The team had little success with either car. Running the M18/22 at the Race of Champions in March 1972 at Brands Hatch, Pilette was slowest in qualifying, a full six seconds behind

Emerson Fittipaldi on pole. Pilette went on to finish 13th, three laps behind Fittipaldi, the eventual winner. A month later in the International Trophy meeting at Silverstone, Pilette finished in 11th place, the race once again being won by Fittipaldi. Probably the only reasonable results for the M22 came in the Tasman series in 1973 where the car was run by a couple of teams, one for driver Howie Sangster.

It seems a shame that such a good looking car should have had such poor results and only ever be know as the last McLaren F5000 car to take to the track.

McLaren M16

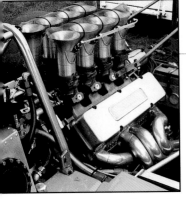

Team McLaren competed in their first Indianapolis races in 1969. They were inspired to enter after listening to radio commentary of Bruce McLaren's long time driving partner Denny Hulme racing a Dan Gurney owned Eagle at the event. The team found it so exciting that they wanted to enter their own cars and the final decision to compete was made in July 1969. The M15 was the first McLaren Indy car and was designed by Gordon Coppuck, based on the team's Can-Am experience. McLaren stuck to their usual race winning methods of testing and re-testing a car until it was not only good but extremely reliable, and within a few months McLaren looked like they could have another winner. Then disaster struck. In a practice session, the fuel cap on Hulme's

car popped open, releasing burning methanol all over driver and car. Methanol flames are invisible, so it took a considerable time for the fire marshals to realize what was happening and come to his aid. Hulme's hands were extremely badly burnt and he was unable to drive for quite a while. Things then got worse, on June 3rd, 1970 Bruce McLaren was killed while testing an M8D Can-Am car at Goodwood. The team decided to deal with this tragic loss by continuing to race in all the major races of the USAC calendar. The M15 performed well but it was soon time to look forward to the new season and design a car taking on board all the lessons Team McLaren had learned in their first year at Indy.

The M16 series of cars were initiated in September 1970 and were first revealed to the press, ready to race, in January 1971 at Team headquarters in Colnbrook, England. The M16 was designed by Coppuck who drew inspiration from the pioneering wedge shaped Lotus Type 72 Formula 1 car. He believed that this car would be good for oval races as the forces applied to the car are a lot more constant than in Formula 1, with only 60mph speed difference between the corners and the straight. The shape was ideal for continuous running but it gave a high level of downthrust at the front which had to be balanced by a large wing at the back.

The tapering monocoque meant the M16 had to have its radiators situated in the middle of the car, alongside the

SPECIFICATIONS

Make: McLaren	Model: M16C
Year: 1973	Color: Orange
Engine: Chevrolet V8	CC: 5815
Power: 710 bhp	Transmission: Hewland LG 500
Brakes: Lockheed Discs	Length: 158"
Width: 74"	Height: 34"
Weight: 1450 lbs	Chassis no: M16C-2
Drivers: Peter Revson	

drivers hips. It also meant that the engine was slung semi-stressed into the monocoque's rear and steadied by tubular A frames at either side. The fuel was stored in the center of the wheelbase to promote lower polar movement. Two speed transmission is normal at Indy but McLaren decided on a Hewland LG500 three speed as it gave better acceleration out of the pits after a pit stop and after yellow light periods.

For the 1973 Indianapolis season McLaren built three M16Cs. The M16C had changed very little from the original M16 apart from the addition of an engine cover to smooth airflow back onto the rear wing. The car loved the fast, open circuits and was very stable at high speeds. The year this McLaren debuted, the M16C began an unparalleled success at the Indy 500.

The M16C-2 in the Mathews collection became Peter Revson's McLaren team car after he had crashed his own chassis at the Indy 500 in 1973. While driving it, he qualified on pole at both Pocono and Ontario. McLaren, as was their standard practice, sold the car to a privateer, Salt Walther at the end of the 1973 season. Walther raced it all through 1974 and 1975 and it then went to David Hobbs in 1976. Jerry Karl purchased the M16C-2 in 1978 as a backup car, converted it to a stock block Chevy V8 and raced in the 1980 Indy where it was placed 21st. Karl ran again at Indy in 1982, with M16C-2 being the oldest McLaren in the field, but it still managed to finish a very respectable 15th.

The McLaren M16 became the most successful car in the history of the Indy 500. Over a ten year period a M16 won three times at the Brickyard, in 1972 driven by Mark Donohue and a M16 driven by Johnny Rutherford was victorious twice, in both 1974 and 1976. 1981 was the final year for a M16 to compete at the Indy 500, it was driven by Vern Schuppan and considering the car designs age finished an extraordinary third. To put this record into perspective during the ten years in which the M16 was running four hundred and fifty cars attempted to even qualify for the Indy 500 and three hundred and twenty competitors actually saw the starting grid. As far as the Mathews collection can ascertain, this is the only complete ex-Team McLaren Indy car in private ownership.

Ford Hot Rods

The phrase 'Hot Rod' has no strict definition although the main aims of 'Hot Rodding' are to make your car bigger, faster, lower and all together more obvious than the next. There are no guidelines or rules on how to build a 'Hot Rod' and improvements and customization can come in a variety of guises, from exotic paint jobs on seriously reworked bodyshells to complete chassis and engine overhauls.

In 1932 Ford finally decided to replace their badly ageing Model A car. Market forces had been causing the Model A's sales to slip and the customers wanted more from their cars, both mechanically and in terms of comfort, so Ford began work on an entirely new car.

The 1932 Ford was an immediate success because it met all the consumer needs including additional luxury and greater power and it also looked elegant. Consequently it sold very well. The 1932 Ford became increasingly commonplace and during the 1940's they were so inexpensive that people began to use them for things such as dirt track racing. This in turn led to people making their own modifications and improvements to the original car.

The 1932 Ford could be described as the quintessential 'Hot Rodding' car and is the most popular of all Hot Rods. It lends itself extremely well to customization with a strong frame and

SPECIFICATIONS

Make: Ford	Model: Hi-Boy
Year: 1932	Color: Black with flames
Engine: Supercharged V8 Chevrolet	CC: 5735
Power: 500 bhp	Transmission: Auto GM
Brakes: Discs	Length: 148"
Width: 70"	Height: 63"
Weight: 2600 lbs	Chassis no: ID41441
Drivers: Billy Gibbons (ZZ Top)	

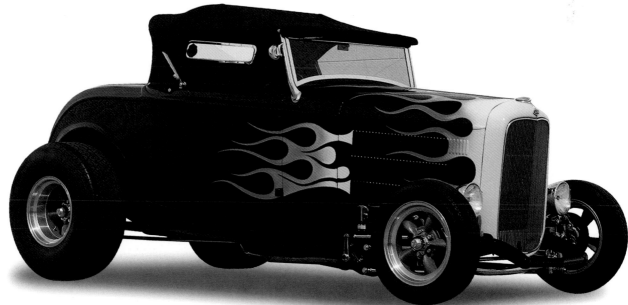

simplicity of build that makes stripping down and modification straightforward. Although the '32 Ford is the most commonly used chassis for Hot Rodding, the whole point is that it is not what you start with but what you make of it that counts.

The Hi-Boy in the Mathews Collection was constructed for Billy Gibbons of rock band 'ZZ Top' fame and was of course built around an original 1932 Ford steel body and frame. The Chevrolet V8 engine is fitted with a Hampton Supercharger for exceptionally high performance and it can run a 1/4 mile in 11 seconds. It is now Harry's favorite Hot Rod, a guaranteed show stopper and a fabulous piece of work.

Boyd Coddington is one of, if not the finest living Hot Rod builder. It is his meticulous attention to detail that makes his creations so great, no imperfection escapes his eye and this is why he consistently builds show winning cars. Coddington became interested in cars at about the age of twelve, and acquired his first vehicle, a 1931 Chevy pick-up truck which he swapped for his shot gun, at the age of fourteen. Before he left school, Coddington had built his first Hot Rod. After receiving his diploma from high school, Coddington took a three year apprenticeship at a machine shop in Salt Lake City and when he was fully trained moved to Los Angeles, California to work as a machinist

for Western Gear. In his spare time he began building Hot Rods and in October 1978 he gave up his paid employment and set up his own full time business. Any worries about making ends meet were soon vanquished, business was rolling in, and word of mouth was spreading the news of Coddington's Hot Rodding skills.

Coddington has not looked back since, his business has continued to grow at a great pace and so has his reputation. People want Boyd Hot Rods for their flawless details and unusual features, and just as importantly, because they come in on time and within the budget. He does not stick to a formula but is always willing to experiment and push the boundaries of what it is possible to do to an automobile. Coddington has won a multitude of awards for his Hot Rods including the Slonaker award in 1981 at the Oakland Roadster Show. At this event in 1982 he won

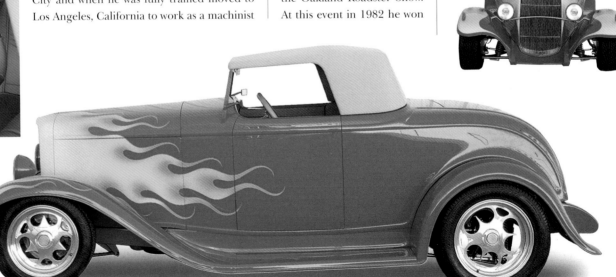

the highly acclaimed accolade: America's Most Beautiful Roadster, a feat which he repeated in 1986 and 1990.

The car in the Mathews Collection was built by Boyd Coddington in 1990. The rear end has a Corvette center section with fabricated axles and linkage anodized to match the body color.

The 1941 gold colored Ford Custom in the Mathews Collection was built as a tribute to the legendary Barris Brothers. The two brothers were customizing heroes who pioneered and contributed to trends for car enthusiasts during the 1940's. The Barris Brothers were true stylists - chopping tops, sectioning and body channelling as well as making other extreme aerodynamic alterations. Like a Barris Brothers' creation, the Mathews car is a one of a kind custom job, which took over thirteen years and cost nearly $200,000 to build. As such a excellent example of personal customization, the car has been featured on the cover of Custom Rodder magazine in May 1994, and at both 'Autorama' and 'World of Wheels' Hot Rod festivals.

All of the customization work was done by Rod Powell in California for the then owners, two executives of CASI (Championship Auto Shows Inc.). He created this Ford Custom from a 1979 Corvette chassis, which he stretched 13" and then hand formed all of the interior. Unfortunately the 1941 Ford Custom is now too valuable to drive and is used only as a show car.

The 'Mini Hi-Boy Hot Rod' on this page was built for Harry's grandson, Luke Burgard, over 13 months. It is a 1/3rd scale replica

SPECIFICATIONS	
Make: Ford	Model: Boyd Coddington Hot Rod
Year: 1932	Color: Red with flames
Engine: Supercharged V8 Chevrolet	CC: 5735
Power: 500 bhp	Transmission: Auto GM
Brakes: Discs	Length: 149"
Width: 67"	Height: 55"
Weight: 2500 lbs	Chassis no: AB0000643
Make: Ford	Model: Custom
Year: 1941	Color: Gold
Engine: Corvette V8	CC: 5735
Power: 220 bhp	Transmission: Auto
Brakes: Discs	Length: 192"
Width: 76"	Height: 51"
Weight: 2800lbs	Chassis no: A195188B

of the 1932 Ford and is powered by a Tecumseh 1 cylinder motor that can achieve 8 bhp and, with long gearing, an amazing top speed of 60 mph. The design and fabrication was done by Greg Jacobs and the body modifications and paintwork by Mark Burgard. The parts came from a variety of sources including several vintage McLaren racecars. It has a snowmobile type torque converter clutch, titanium rotor, Wildwood brake calliper, roll cage, 4-point harness, dual exhausts and boat trailer axles and hubs, quite a machine for a seven year old!

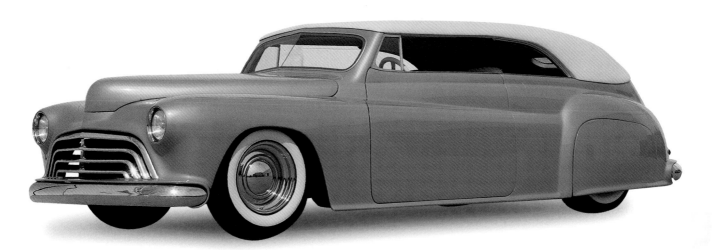

Mercury & Nash

The 1950 Mercury is a classic American Hot Rodding car and was often customized. The Mercury in the Mathews collection is an example of 'Lead Sled' modification which means lead filler is used to create the unusual contours. The door handles are filled in and the body shaping around the headlights has been done with lead in this manner. The subframe on the Mercury is from a later Chevrolet Camaro and the car is fitted with a GM automatic transmission.

The top has been dropped by 4 inches, reducing the already small window area significantly and in line with 1950's customization practice, all the chromework has been removed as has the original sliced sausage grill.

It is certainly unusual to make a Nash into a Hot Rod and the one in the Mathews Collection is not only a Hot Rod/Custom car but is also a pro-street drag racer. It has been built from a 2x3 box frame that has been tubbed in the rear, which means that

SPECIFICATIONS

Make: Mercury	Model: Two door sedan
Year: 1950	Color: Black with Flames
Engine: Chevrolet V8	CC: 5735
Power: 180 bhp	Transmission: 3 speed GM auto
Brakes: Discs	Length: 200"
Width: 77"	Height: 58"
Weight: 3200 lbs	Chassis no: 50SL64454
Drivers: n/a	

the axle has been narrowed so that wider tires could be added. This particular Nash has 4 bar suspension and a Mustang II front end. The covered front wheels do actually offer some degree of steering!

The Nash in the Mathews Collection is certainly a true competition car and is thus fitted with a roll cage for serious drag racing, as well as a GM Turbo 350 automatic transmission, just the right ticket for a fast getaway.

SPECIFICATIONS

Make: Nash	Model: Pinin Farina Coupe
Year: 1954	Color: Red with yellow flames
Engine: Chevrolet V8	CC: 5340
Power: 350 bhp	Transmission: GM Auto
Brakes: Discs	Length: 184"
Width: 75"	Height: 55"
Weight: 3200 lbs	Chassis no: D171882
Drivers: n/a	

Austin Healey 100M

The Austin Healey is an absolute classic British sports car. The Healey 100 was launched in the Earls Court Motor Show in October 1952 where Len Lord, the chairman of Austin, offered to take over its manufacture and marketing. The car was renamed the Austin Healey 100 and the base price was reduced from £850 to £750. This first Austin-Healey car has become known as the 100-4 or the BN-1 and 10,688 units were built. It was fitted with an Austin A90, 2660cc, four cylinder engine, which gave 94 bhp. The three speed gearbox was also sourced from the A90, but had first gear blanked off and overdrive fitted on second and third to give extra power.

The BN2 was launched in October 1955 and in total 3,924 units were built. The BN2 had a simple box frame chassis and was basically the same as the BN1, but fitted with larger drum brakes and a completely new four speed gearbox with overdrive as standard. The BN designation can be broken down to describe the car, the 'B' stood for the B class engine, which meant it had a

capacity between 2000 and 3000cc. The 'N' was the letter issued for an open topped two seater. The engine was basically an unstressed truck unit so was excellent for reliability and high mileages. It is capable of going for around two hundred thousand miles before wear necessitates a complete overhaul.

By the time the BN2 was released, the Austin-Healey 100S, a limited production run of 55 racing cars, was becoming well known for its ability at circuit rallying and racing. This led to the production of the Le Mans 100M variation of the BN2 and this Le

SPECIFICATIONS

Make: Austin Healey	Model: 100M
Year: 1955	Color: Black & white
Engine: 4 cylinders	CC: 2600
Power: 110 bhp	Transmission: 4 speed w OD
Brakes: Drum	Length: 148"
Width: 56"	Height: 38"
Weight: 2160 lbs	Chassis no: BNIL225762
Drivers: n/a	

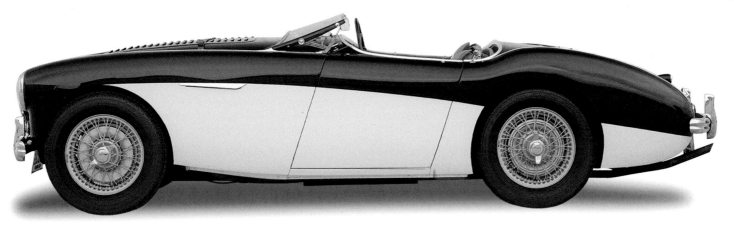

Mans specification kit was only available with the BN2. The engine power was increased from 90 bhp to either 100 or 110 bhp, depending on the camshaft fitted. The Le Mans kits also had bigger carburettors and changes were made to the distributor, valve springs and a stiffened front anti roll bar was added; approximately 1100 of the Le Mans BN2s were originally made and an extra one hundred were later modified.

The Austin-Healey 100M in the Mathews Collection is a member of the Le Mans registry, this means it has been converted to Le Mans configuration. To be registered, the car must have a minimum specification of 1.75 inch H 6. S.U. carburettors, be fitted with special inlet manifolds, cold air box and air tube, a factory style louvered hood and a Le Mans regulation strap. The 100M is finished in duo-tone paint as was standard for the 100M at that time.

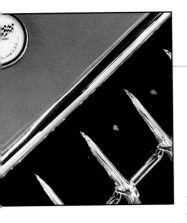

Corvette

The prototype Corvette had its first public outing in January 1953 and the car was in mass production by June of that year. A new Corvette model has been put on sale every year since then, but in the Corvette's 48 years of production there have only been five different basic body shapes. This car is an example of the original body shape, which was built between 1953 and 1955.

In 1954, sales figures were expected to peak at 10,000 units but had only reached a disappointing 3,640, leaving over 1,000 units unsold at the start of 1955. Figures for '55 were so dramatically low that the future of the whole Corvette project was put in jeopardy and a total of only 700 units were built, the second lowest ever annual production total for the Corvette.

What the Corvette needed was better performance and handling. Back in 1952, Chevrolet's chief engineer Ed Cole, along with Harry Barr had begun to work on an all new Chevrolet V8 for their passenger car range, and in 1955 this V8 engine found its way under the Corvette's hood. The new engine proved to be the Corvette's savior and made its transition into a true sports car complete.

Most, but not all, 1955 Corvettes have the Chevrolet V8 engine, and there are several ways to tell. The chassis number is the major indication, chassis numbers that start with a 'V' are genuine V8 engined cars, while for all six cylinder models the 'V' is omitted. Another tell tale sign of the true engine specification is in the Chevrolet script on both front fenders, those with the V8 engine have a large gold 'V' attached over the smaller 'v' script.

The Corvette in the Mathews Collection is of course an example of the V8 model, the champion of the Corvette name. The 1955 Corvette model was only available in five colors, Polo White, Pennant Blue, Corvette Copper, Harvest Gold and as seen on the Mathew's car, Gypsy Red.

SPECIFICATIONS

Make: Chevrolet	Model: Corvette
Year: 1955	Color: Red
Engine: Chevrolet V8	CC: 4343
Power: 195 bhp	Transmission: 3 Speed automatic
Brakes: Drum	Length: 167"
Width: 70"	Height: 52"
Weight: 2900 lbs	Chassis no: VE55S001545
Drivers: n/a	

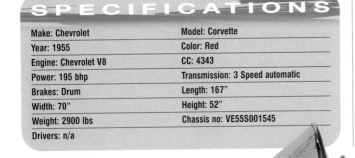

Devin MG special

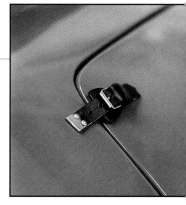

The Devin marque was created by Bill Devin, a Californian kit car pioneer and enthusiast who was born in 1915 in Rocky, Oklahoma and died on November 22nd, 2000. From an early age Devin was around cars and his deep rooted interest in them was bred into him by his mechanic father. Devin was an innovator and he devised the first belt driven overhead camshaft four cylinder

engine. Drawing on his wealth of manual and intellectual skills he built the most successful 'specials' of the late 1950's.

Devin was instinctively drawn to motor racing and in 1951, driving a Devin built Crosley Special, he won the first event he entered. Devin's success with the Crosley spurred him on further and he moved on to racing a Ferrari 212 that his close friend Phil Hill had driven in the

1952 Carrera Pan American. Devin soon started acquiring more Ferraris and other cars and in 1956 he won the SCCA National Championship in a Devin Panhard sports car. Shortly after this victory, Devin started producing replicas and roadster kits for sale.

SPECIFICATIONS

Make: Devin	Model: Devin Special
Year: 1957	Color: Red
Engine: Chevrolet V8	CC: 4640
Power: 220 bhp	Transmission: Chevrolet 4 speed
Brakes: Discs	Length: 149"
Width: 62"	Height: 39"
Weight: 2100 lbs	Chassis no: HDR4325922
Drivers: n/a	

In 1952, a trip to Italy would prove to be the greatest influence on all of the cars that Devin later built. Visiting the Ferrari factory allowed Devin access to the information required for correctly setting up a Ferrari for racing and during this time he also discussed the possibility of converting a single seat Ferrari Formula 1 car to a two seater sports car. Another factor that facilitated Devin's success was fiberglass. In the early 1950's it had just started to become a viable option for the construction of car bodies. Devin devised a modular system of moulds, allowing him to make bodies for chassis varying from 76" in length to 106", dramatically improving marketability. The Devin kits were the first mould to have a cockpit with the seats and transmission cover built in. Devin's work never received the acclaim it deserved and he became disillusioned, eventually quitting the motoring scene in 1964.

The Devin Special in the Mathews Collection started life as an MGA, the frame of which was covered with the lightweight Devin imitation Ferrari Testa Rosa body. Power is provided by a Chevrolet V8 engine with three Stromberg 97s and Chevrolet 4 speed transmission.

MGA TC

The MGA first came onto the market in 1955. It was a complete break from the past for MG, a departure from the pre-war look of the company's sports cars. Straight lines gave way to the obvious benefits of streamlining. The body looked modern, with the fenders blending into the body work to create a beautiful and aerodynamic shape. The MGA's long curvaceous lines have definitely stood the test of time.

SPECIFICATIONS

Make: MG	Model: MGA Twin Cam
Year: 1959	Color: Beige
Engine: 4 Cylinder Twin cam	CC: 1588
Power: 108 bhp	Transmission: 4 speed manual
Brakes: Dunlop Discs	Length: 152"
Width: 56"	Height: 43"
Weight: 2200lbs	Chassis no: YD32202
Drivers: n/a	

Before the MGA was officially launched, three prototypes - named EX.182 - were entered into the 1955 Le Mans race. The cars did exceptionally well and finished fifth and sixth in their class. The MGA was introduced in September 1955 with an already proven competition history only adding to its appeal. Despite its controversial styling, the

MGA became the best ever selling MG prior to the ceasing of production in 1962 and the launch of the all conquering MGB.

The MGA chassis was a development of the TD Midget's unit, with wider spaced side rails for a lower seating position to accommodate the new lower bodywork and made from a steel frame with box section main side members, cross braces and scuttle bracing structures. The seating position was not only more suited to the new sportscar image but also helped to lower the center of gravity of the car, thus improving its cornering capabilities.

The MGA Twin Cam variation was announced in April 1958 and remained in limited production until April 1960. In total, 2111 Twin Cams were produced, all of which were open two seaters and essentially aimed at competition use. Visually, the Twin Cam did not vary much from the standard MGA model apart from its special steel disc wheels, replacing the previously used wires.

However, under the bonnet there was a world of difference. The cylinder block and bottom end were bored out and strengthened standard 'B' series components, but the cylinder head was a new aluminum unit incorporating twin overhead camshafts. Twin SU carburettors were fitted as standard which gave the Twin Cam a power out put of 110 bhp, a 0-60 time of 11.5 seconds and a top speed of 115 mph. With all the additional power available the standard MGA drum brakes were replaced by Dunlop discs all around.

Producing a twin cam engine version of the MGA had originally been the idea of designer Gerald Palmer. However, the engine was eventually designed by Austin Motor Cars. The main advantage of using a modified version of the regular engine was that it would easily fit with the standard MGA gearbox and into the unmodified engine bay. The redesign proved incredibly successful and greatly improved the engine, although it was prone to damage through over revving.

'61 Corvette

I n 1961 the Corvette was still the only mass produced sports car manufactured in America. Edward N. Cole, the chief executive of General Motors, had developed the Corvette with engineer Zora Arkus-Duntov, who originally wanted the car to progress on separate racing and touring lines. This did not happen, and after 1957, Chevrolet decided to combine the comfort of a tourer with the ability of a competition sports car. The first Corvette to demonstrate this philosophy was the 1960 Corvette and these ideas grew and matured into the 1961 model. In their review of the the 1961 Corvette 'Sports Car Illustrated' described the car as "one of the most remarkable marriages of touring comfort and violent performance we have ever enjoyed" reflecting Corvettes success in fulfiling this vision.

The styling for the 1961 Corvette was new; it did not have any 'teeth' in the grill and had four tail lights, a look which would become the tradition. It had a new back-end shape that blended in seamlessly with the original body shape. These changes were derived from the Sting Ray, the GM Racing Corvette owned by Bill Mitchell. The 1961 model was the first Corvette to have exhaust exits below the body, which angled outwards just behind the rear wheels instead of going through the bumper tips. The radiator and top tank were both aluminum and this tank, separated from the radiator, allowed for a more graceful hood slope. The 1961 Corvette had new upholstery with narrow ribbing, increasing the overall feeling of being in a true sports car but with a plush touring car interior.

Handling and performance were also improved on the 1961 Corvette. The car sat flatter than before, had a lower center of gravity and moderately stiff suspension for easy cornering. There were now five different engine options, all based on a 283 cubic inch displacement which, starting with a single four barrel carburettor engine giving 230 bhp, went up to a 315 bhp fuel injection, special camshaft engine.

Production for the year 1961 was around 10,939. Of these, 954 were painted in the same colors as the car in the Mathews Collection, the body in Roman Red and the cove in white. 1961 was the last year that contrasting cove color was available for the Corvette. Of the large number of Corvettes in his collection, this is certainly Harry's favorite.

SPECIFICATIONS

Make: Chevrolet	Model: Corvette
Year: 1961	Color: Red
Engine: Chevrolet V8	CC: 4638
Power: 315 bhp	Transmission: 4 speed
Brakes: Drum	Length: 177"
Width: 73"	Height: 52"
Weight: 3035 lbs	Chassis no: 10867S102758
Drivers: n/a	

Ferrari 250 Lusso

The Lusso premiered at the Paris Motor Show in October 1962 as the Ferrari 250GT Berlinetta Lusso (Lusso meaning luxury). It was manufactured between January 1963 and August 1964 and during this time a mere 350 cars were produced, with each unit taking approximately three months to build.

The Lusso is widely regarded as Ferrari's most beautiful car; its long fluid flowing lines were wonderfully designed by

hood and trunk. The gearbox is front mounted; rear mounted gearboxes were not fitted in Ferraris until the 275GTB. The front suspension is wishbone and coil, the rear semi-elliptic leaf springs with parallel trailing arms and Watt's linkage.

Internally the Lusso is light and airy, its thin pillars and big windows allow the driver a barely interrupted view in every direction. This superb visibility is an essential in a car which has no external mirrors to ruin its beautiful lines! The seats are of genuine sports car design with the buckets hugging the hips as the

Pinin Farina and built by Scaglietti. The chromework is subtle with a small front bumper and nudgebars just below the sidelights. The Lusso was described by 'Car & Driver' in May 1964 "...its proportions approach perfection." Not only did it look amazing but the Lusso had a top speed of around 150mph, with a 0-60 time of 8.0 seconds and 0-100 in 19.5. The external design may be a classic but the dashboard layout is certainly not. The all important speedometer and tachometer are in the center of the dash, out of the direct line of sight of the driver. Having said, that the dash is simple and clean, although it does have a row of unidentified switches.

The chassis is tubular and strengthened by two longerons while the body is mainly steel with aluminum panels for the doors,

car corners. The driving position is with bent knees, the handling and roadholding being truly 1960's.

The Mathews Lusso is dark blue with a tan leather interior. It is as close to priceless art on wheels as you can get.

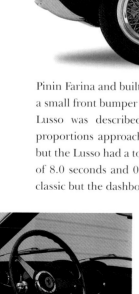

SPECIFICATIONS

Make: Ferrari	Model: 250 GTL Lusso
Year: 1964	Color: Blue
Engine: V12	CC: 2953
Power: 250 bhp	Transmission: 4 speed
Brakes: Discs	Length: 173"
Width: 71"	Height: 51"
Weight: 3270	Chassis no: 5141
Drivers: n/a	

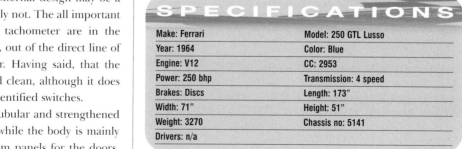

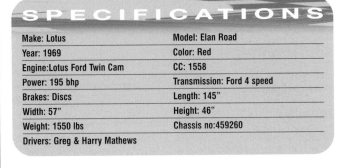

" The Giant Killer Street Car "

The Elan was years ahead of any other British sports car. It was introduced by Lotus in 1962 as the successor of the financially disastrous Elite. One of the features that had made the Elite so unprofitable was its monocoque bodyshell and Colin Chapman, the legendary innovator behind the Lotus marque, needed to find a replacement. The solution was the Elan with its backbone chassis, a feature which would become a Lotus hallmark for many years. The design of the Elan was not as puritan as the Elite due to the fact that Lotus compromised its rigid styling to fall in line with production viability and costs.

The backbone chassis was made of 18 gauge steel with localized 16 gauge stiffening and weighed a mere 75lbs. Cross members and turrets at the front cradled the engine, gearbox, steering and suspension. The rear housed the final drive and suspension. The body was designed by Ron Hickman and was moulded in two main fiberglass sections, the floorpan/arches and upper body, which were then bonded together. Additional steel strengthening for the door jams and windshield pillars made it sufficiently rigid so as not to rely on the chassis for all its strength. The clean

SPECIFICATIONS

Make: Lotus	Model: Elan Road
Year: 1969	Color: Red
Engine: Lotus Ford Twin Cam	CC: 1558
Power: 195 bhp	Transmission: Ford 4 speed
Brakes: Discs	Length: 145"
Width: 57"	Height: 46"
Weight: 1550 lbs	Chassis no: 459260
Drivers: Greg & Harry Mathews	

aerodynamic lines suggested the need for pop up headlights and these were activated by a vacuum system ingeniously utilizing the chassis as a air chamber.

The Elan quickly gained a reputation as an ultra responsive, balanced and quick car, and in its first year it attracted over 2000 customers. Its success almost certainly saved Lotus from an early demise. Its popularity was due to the fact that the Elan was beyond compare to anything else on the market at the time, especially in its price range. For sheer cornering power, acceleration and driver involvement it was in a class of its own. The Elan S2 arrived in November 1964 with several small improvements including larger front callipers, full width polished veneer dash with a lockable glovebox, quick release filler cap and new rear lenses.

There was, however, some criticism of some of the more 'down to earth' aspects of owning the Elan, and Lotus introduced a closed coupe model in 1965, the Series 3 Elan. A drophead

SPECIFICATIONS

Make: Lotus	Model: Elan Race
Year: 1964	Color: Red
Engine: Lotus Ford Twin Cam	CC: 1558
Power: 195 bhp	Transmission: Ford 4 speed
Brakes: Discs	Length: 145"
Width: 56"	Height: 43"
Weight: 1375 lbs	Chassis no: 26/4450
Drivers: Greg & Harry Mathews	

version of the S3 was introduced in June 1966 and was built until March 1968 when it was superseded by the Series 4 convertible. The most significant S4 changes were: flared squared off wheel arches to accommodate wider, low profile 155/13 radial tires, larger rear tail lights and a hood bulge to clear the new Stromberg carburettors Federalised versions of the Elan S4 had Zenith-Stromberg carburation with cross-over exhaust pipes in the engine bay. They also had one large wheel nut instead of knock-on ears, side turn signal lights on the front and rear fenders and a door mounted 'Bullet' rear view mirror. Production of the Elan finally ended in August 1973 with a grand total of over 9000 produced.

The Mathews family have been Lotus enthusiasts and racers for many years, and the Elan has always been one of their favorites. There are currently three beautiful examples of the Elan in their collection, two are racing versions of the S1, the other is a modified road going S4. The two S1 cars are full spec. stripped out lightweight race cars that can only be told apart by the gold bumpers on number 9. All the members of the Mathews family have had victories in these cars at circuits everywhere the USA, and above all else they have great fun racing against each other in the Elans.

Harry Mathews refers to the 1969 Elan as the "Giant Killer". It is a stock looking Elan but is actually highly modified with a Spyder tubular steel chassis and full Spyder suspension. The engine is a full race spec. 195 bhp Twin Cam and has a larger radiator, billet axles and a limited slip differential. The consequences of these and other performance upgrades mean that the little Elan is capable of a top speed of 140 mph and on classic car rallies all around the USA leaves the surprised drivers of older Ferraris for dead. The best way to describe this car is light and quick with extremely good handling - a wolf in sheep's clothing!

Jaguar E-Type

" Arguably the prettiest sports car ever built "

The Jaguar XKE or E-Type, as it become known, was unveiled by Sir William Lyons at the Geneva Show in March 1961. In its original form, it came with a 3.8 litre 265 bhp engine which was enlarged at the end of 1964 to 4.2 litres when the bore was increased from 87mm to 92mm. At the same time, the gearbox was upgraded to a 4-speed all synchromesh type and the clutch certainly had enough bite to get the E-Type quickly off the mark with a 0-60 time of just 7.4 seconds.

The other major upgrade that came at the same time as the new engine was the new suspension. The front suspension was fairly standard for its time, but at the back the E-Type was the first car to use the four coil independent system designed by Bill Heynes and Bob Knight. The system they designed had parallel lower links each side and utilized the half shaft as the upper suspension link. It was this new suspension that set the E-type apart from its more expensive competition, allowing the drive to remain smooth even at high speeds. This suspension was so successful that its basic principles are still in use today at Jaguar. Brake discs were brought inboard at the rear and the footwells were deepened to increase ease of access and comfort.

The E-Type body was designed by Jaguar's aerodynamicist Malcolm Sayer, as a longer, finless road going interpretation of the D-type racing car. He drew the designs for his cars on 20 foot lengths of paper pinned to the wall, creating curves from which three dimensional co-ordinates could be worked out. Drawing on the valuable experience acquired through his work at the Bristol Airplane Corporation, Sayer tested everything in the wind tunnel at RAF Farnborough to optimize high speed stability and minimize drag.

driveshaft tunnel and across the car in the form of cross members. The engine, front suspension, steering and hood are mounted on the narrow tubular front sub-frame.

The most distinctive feature of the E-Type is its remarkable nose which hangs a long way out from the 96" wheelbase. The E-Type is not only fantastic looking from every angle but was the fastest production sports car of its time. The styling made little concession to fashions of the time, yet it is very much of its time. No other car reflects the UK in the sixties as much as the E-Type; for as little as £1500, people could buy themselves an extraordinary sports car and drive up and down the newly opened and as yet unrestricted motorways at the E-Types stunning top speed of a quoted 141mph. The Series 1 4.2 open top was produced for four years with a total production of 9,540, of which 8,490 were exported, mainly to the USA.

Aircraft principles were used to make the stressed and welded steel monocoque style main tub which contains the passengers and forms the major part of the body. The body is braced by box sections along the door sills, around the scuttle, along the

SPECIFICATIONS

Make: Jaguar	Model: XKE
Year: 1966	Color: Red
Engine: 6 Cylinder Twin Cam	CC: 4235
Power: 265 bhp	Transmission: 4 speed manual
Brakes: Discs	Length: 174"
Width: 63"	Height: 42"
Weight: 2960 lbs	Chassis no: 1E12302
Drivers: n/a	

AC Cobra 427

"Yes, its a real one!"

The Cobra 427 has its roots very firmly planted in the British company A.C.'s open topped sports car, the Ace. The tubular framed Ace sports car was introduced in 1954 with all independent suspension designed by John Tojeiro. In 1963, Carroll Shelby, Cobra's founder, adopted this car and developed it with disc brakes all around and a 4.7 litre Ford engine which delivered 330 bhp. In 1966 the larger Cobra 427, with its 7 litre Ford engine, was added to the range.

Shelby wanted to build a car with a chassis from England and an engine from the USA; with this idea in mind, he became acquainted with the late Charles Hurlock and his nephew Derek, who ran A.C. Cars of Thames Ditton in Surrey, England. A.C. had just lost their suppliers of 6 cylinder Bristol engines for the Ace, and Shelby offered to continue paying them to produce the Ace chassis for his own sports car, to which he would add an American V8 engine and gearbox. A.C. provisionally accepted his offer as long as a suitable engine could be found. Shelby's proposal took a

step closer to fruition in October 1961 when Ford introduced their 221ci small block engine. Shelby contacted Ford with regard to his idea and the possibility of acquiring this engine and Ford expressed a serious interest in his project.

The first Ace chassis arrived in the USA in February 1962, Shelby installed a 260 ci HiPo engine and Borg-Warner four speed gearbox, and the first AC Cobra was created. This may have been the first, but the prototype Cobra, designated the CSX 2000, made its debut at the New York Auto Show in April 1962. The CSX 2000 appeared on the Ford stand where it attracted a lot of attention and dealers started placing orders. Shelby committed himself full time to his Cobra project and more chassis' were shipped over from A.C. Cars. The company was, however, having teething problems, the chassis' needed extensive upgrades and alterations and Shelby could not build them fast enough. The prototype CSX 2000 was constantly painted different colors for magazine reviews to give the impression of a substantial quantity of cars being produced.

The Cobra was given its Federation Internationale de L'Automobile classification as a GT III car in August 1962. This

meant the car could compete in the over two litre class of the FIA Manufacturer Championship. The Cobra was given this classification even though only eight cars were completed and the FIA rules stated that a minimum of one hundred units had to be completed to meet the FIA standards. The Cobra's first FIA race was the Los Angeles Grand Prix on the 13th October 1962, and it was driven by Bill Krause. Krause drove a good race and led for a time until the rear hub broke and he had to retire. For Riverside, January 1963, the rear hubs was strengthened and two Cobras, driven by Dave MacDonald and Ken Miles, were entered. MacDonald came first and Miles second, well ahead of the Corvettes, their nearest rivals.

Shelby ran his first Le Mans 24 hours in a Cobra in 1963. Ford refused to provide him with an engine so, with the help of A.C. Cars and Ed Hugus, Shelby prepared his own cars, one for himself to drive and one which Hugus drove. The fastest Cobra managed

SPECIFICATIONS

Make: Shelby Cobra	Model: 427
Year: 1967	Color: Blue with white stripe
Engine: Ford V8	CC: 6998
Power: 425 bhp	Transmission: Ford 4 speed
Brakes: Girling Discs	Length: 156"
Width: 71"	Height: 49"
Weight: 2460 lbs	Chassis no: CSX3356
Drivers: n/a	

to finish an extremely respectable seventh overall. Cobra's impressive race history continued at the Bridgehampton 500km race in September 1963 where Dan Gurney drove a Cobra to victory, and in doing so, he became the first ever American driver to win an FIA race in an American car. The Shelby Cobras returned to the Le Mans 24 hour race in 1964 and completely eclipsed the previous years results by coming fourth overall and first in the GT section, defeating the dominant Ferraris.

The prototype of the new version of the car, the Cobra '427' was built in November 1964 and the official press launch was in January 1965 at the Riverside International Raceway. The Cobra 427 had a new tubular coil spring chassis created by Ford engineer Klaus Arning, who, basing his ideas on the design of the original Ace, developed a suitable platform for the higher power of the big block Cobra. The bodywork was also modernized giving it a much more macho appearance with flared arches. The Cobra 427 was capable of incredible speed, going from zero to one hundred and back to zero in less than thirteen seconds. Production began in April 1965 but ground to a halt in March 1967 after approximately 160 road cars had been built, one of which is the Cobra 427 in the Mathews Collection, an excellent example that has never been raced.

'67 Corvette

In its entire history the Corvette has had five major body re-styles. The 1967 Corvette was produced for the fifth and final year of the body style created in 1963. The 1967 Corvette bodystyling had little planning. Chevrolet had wanted to introduce a new body shape in 1967 based on the Mako Shark Stingray, but production problems delayed the new shape and the Corvette group had to create something new from the four year old body. The designers removed trim, including the hood script emblem and fender flags to clean up body surfaces. The functional side fender vents were replaced with a new style which had five slots and the gas cap color was altered to match the body. Internally the car had new upholstery and redesigned seats. The emergency hand brake was repositioned to be center mounted, a Corvette first.

The 1967 Corvette came with a choice of seven different engines sizes, from the smallest 300 bhp 327 cubic inch (5360cc) small block to the big block 427 cubic inch (6997cc) L88 engine. The massive V8 427 cubic inch engine was added to the Corvette range after they started losing races to the AC Cobras. With this new engine the 1967 Corvette could do 0-60 in 4.7 seconds and 0-100 in a mere 12.3 seconds.

When it was originally produced, the 1967 Corvette was not as popular as previous models as the public were waiting for the new model, but still the 1967 Corvette had a total production run of 22,940 units of which 8,504 were coupes and 14,436 were convertibles.

The Sunfire Yellow 1967 427 Corvette in the Mathews collection is certainly a beautiful example of this unpopular at the time Corvette shape. It is one of 2,325 in this color and it is used only as a show car and has won many awards at shows across the States. In 1997 the car received the NCRS-Duntov Mark of Excellence Award from the National Corvette Restorers Society; it is its greatest accolade and it is the ultimate concours award for a Corvette.

SPECIFICATIONS

Make: Chevrolet	Model: Corvette
Year: 1967	Color: Yellow
Engine: Chevrolet V8	CC: 6998
Power: 435 bhp	Transmission: 4 speed automatic Powerglide
Brakes: Discs	Length: 175"
Width: 70"	Height: 50"
Weight: 3400 lbs	Chassis no: 194677S100776
Drivers: n/a	

Ferrari 330 GTS

The Ferrari 330 GTC was unveiled at the Geneva Salon in March 1966. The 330 GTC (Gran Turismo Coupe) was a union of the 275 GTB chassis and the basic engine from the 330 GT 2+2. The "open topped" Spyder version of the 330 was not introduced until the Paris Motor Show of May 1966, although it had actually been completed several months before the introduction of the GTC. Only a limited run of around 100 of the GT Spyder were ever produced

Ferrari's engineers who worked on the 330 GTS managed to solve the alignment problems that had affected Ferrari's earlier 275 series of cars. They introduced a torque tube which formed a solid link between the front mounted engine and the rear mounted transaxle. This arrangement drastically reduced the number of engine mounting points and thus a new engine became necessary. The Tipo 209/66 was introduced exclusively for the GTC/S and was an all new unit with a revised cylinder block.

The 330 GTS is a combination of a 400 SuperAmerica front blended with a 275 GTS rear tail and the elegant body was designed and built by Pininfarina. To many, the 330 GTS was and is still one of the finest road going Ferraris ever built, the ultimate Gran Turismo. Not only does the 330 GTS look amazing, it handles well, and is fast, quiet and comfortable. It has an incredible top speed of a touch over 150 mph.

This is Harry Mathews' favorite older Ferrari. It has the combination of beautiful styling, a comfortable and roomy interior and the great sounding V12 engine that gives one an all round exciting driving experience. Harry frequently drives this car at vintage rallies all over the USA and for these very reasons, long distance journeys certainly prove no problem.

SPECIFICATIONS

Make: Ferrari	Model: 330 GTS
Year: 1967	Color: Red
Engine: V12	CC: 3967
Power: 300 bhp	Transmission: 5 speed
Brakes: Servo asst Discs	Length: 174"
Width: 66"	Height: 49"
Weight: 3450 lbs	Chassis no: 10845
Drivers: n/a	

Chevron B-16

" One of the best looking race cars ever built "

The Chevron marque was the brainchild of designer Derek Bennett. He drove his first ever Chevron design, the Chevron B1, in a Clubman Formula event on July 3rd, 1965 where he finished first overall, the start of a long history of successes.

The Chevron B16 was an evolution of the B8 which had been Bennett's GT car for three years, evolving over time to meet his customer's needs. He wanted to put all the knowledge he had acquired over that time into a new car and began work on the B16 prototype early in 1969.

The B16 spaceframe chassis is reinforced with steel and duraluminum sheeting to form a full monocoque in the central section. Tubular frames were attached to carry the front suspension, mid-mounted engine and the gearbox unit. Bennett continued with his philosophy of keeping his cars simple but refined enough to work to their maximum, and the B16 includes no major technical innovations, but for ease of maintenance it did have a removable front subframe. Suspension is by double wishbones at the front and upper link and triangular wishbones at the rear. The B16's body shape is basically Bennett's design but he called in the help of stylist Jim Clark, an employee at Specialist Mouldings, to help him with the final details of the shapely fiberglass body.

SPECIFICATIONS

Make: Chevron	Model: B-16
Year: 1969	Color: Blue with red stripe
Engine: Cosworth FVC	CC: 2200
Power: 300bhp	Transmission: Hewland FT200
Brakes: Discs	Length: 155"
Width: 70"	Height: 37"
Weight: 1300 lbs	Chassis no: B16DBE21
Drivers: n/a	

For the engine, Bennett went to see Cosworth, whose 1598cc FVA Formula 2 engine had powered the B8. Bennett wanted the engine increased to nearer 2 litres and Keith Duckworth, Cosworth's main engineer, could see there was a place in the increasingly popular sports car scene for this size engine. So, using a different crank and longer stroke they increased the FVA's capacity to 1790cc, giving 245 bhp and designated it the FVC.

Bennett's eagerly awaited Chevron B16 made its debut in a test session at Aintree in July 1969, where it ran within the lap record. From this promising start, and another excellent outing at Croft, Bennett decided that the B16's first official event should be at the Nurburgring 500km race on 7th September 1969. The B16 was driven by Brian Redman and powered by a Cosworth 1600cc FVA Formula 2 engine. The combination worked well and the B16 qualified on pole, a massive 5.6 seconds faster than the nearest contender. Redman led the race from the start and during the three and a half hour event, never lost his position. The combination had worked, Chevron were victorious.

After such an amazing start, other drivers came looking for a B16 but many found it hard to drive with its huge amount of understeer. The real problem was that there was not enough downforce at the rear, so the B16 gained the two 'orange box' rear spoilers it would have when it went into proper production. Regardless of these problems, orders were still flooding in. The B16 did not race in England until 15th March 1970 and did not win until two weeks later when John Burton won a round of the RAC British Sports Car Championship. Chevron began looking to the new European 2 litre Sports Car series. The extremely talented Redman was again the B16 driver, and the team were enthused until they got to the opening event and saw the brand new Lola T210. Redman knew he would have to work hard during the race and he and the Lola were soon separated from the rest of the pack. Redman fought all the way, and after the Lola took an unexpected pitstop for fuel, he went on to victory. After battling against the Lola at many meetings and time and again being beaten, Redman begged Bennett for a open car. It was an inevitable request, and as the initial order rush for the B16 had subsided, Bennett was now able to go to work on an open version.

The B16 coupe is one of the best looking race cars ever built and it still has the same 'wow' factor now as it did then. The whole car is beautiful and the B16's long, flowing lines are amazingly graceful. This Chevron Coupe, of which only twenty three were built, was very successful in endurance racing, although according to Harry, it is actually too hot to race in the summer as its closed design makes the internal temperature uncomfortable.

Brabham BT35

> **My all time favorite race car to drive**

Jack Brabham was a second generation Australian. His greengrocer father taught him to drive at the age of twelve, and after spending two years in the Air Force, Jack set up a small repairs business. It was while here that he was approached by American Johnny Schonberg, a midget car driver, to build him a car. Brabham did so, but not before Schonberg was talked out of competitive racing by his wife. This

SPECIFICATIONS

Make: Brabham	Model: BT-35
Year: 1971	Color: Red and gold
Engine: Lotus Twin Cam	CC: 1600
Power: 190	Transmission: Hewland FT200
Brakes: Girling Discs	Length: 143"
Width: 74"	Height: 36"
Weight: 1100 lbs	Chassis no: BT35-19
Drivers: n/a	

left Brabham with his own car and he decided to have a go for himself. His debut was at Paramatta Park Speedway and he was bitten by the bug. He entered the New South Wales Championship and in his first season Brabham was victorious. During his time spent on the local circuits, Brabham met Ron Tauranac and formed a partnership that would last and take them both to Europe and to Formula 1.

In 1955 Brabham came to England for his GP debut at Aintree and soon joined the Cooper works team. Initially, he thrived at Cooper and in 1959 won the World Championship in a Cooper with a 2.5 litre Coventry Climax engine. In 1960, Brabham repeated this feat, his overall victory including an impressive five straight wins. Although he was triumphing at Cooper, Brabham was not happy and felt stifled. He took the decision to join up with Ron Tauranac and in 1961 formed Motor Racing Developments. They built one car, retaining the company name MRD, but gave their cars the marque name Brabham. The aim was to build single seater and sports racing cars alongside a F1 team effort. Brabham's rise during the mid sixties was meteoric and when in 1966, the new 3 litre Formula 1 came into existence, Jack, in his own car powered by an Australian Repco Company engine, won the

World Drivers Championship Championship. He thus became the first driver to do so in a car bearing his own name. The following year the Brabham name was again victorious, this time in the hands of Denny Hulme. The partnership lasted until 1971 when Brabham finally sold his share and returned to Australia.

During this tremendously successful period in Formula 1, the company still managed to produce highly competitive customer cars such as the BT-35 which came in three different versions, all produced during 1971. The BT-35A was the American SCCA version of the car and is distinguished by its inboard rear brakes and Hewland FT 200 gearbox. Only three of these cars were ever built and were supplied with Ford 1600 Twin Cam engines. The BT-35B is the Formula B/Atlantic version of the same car, of which a mere seven were built. This is the variation of the BT-35 in the Mathews Collection. It has 13x10 front and 13x14 inch rear tires, has outboard rear brakes along with the Hewland FT200 gearbox and is fitted with a Lotus Twin Cam engine. The largest production run was of the Formula 3 BT-35C of which twenty

seven were made. These had Hewland Mark 8 gearboxes.

All of the three of the BT-35 variations are built in basically the same manner. The chassis is a bronze welded tubular steel space frame with the cockpit made from steel sheet panels. The body is formed from three resin bonded fiberglass sections; the nose, separate from the cockpit section, and the undertray. This was the last Brabham to be built with a tubular chassis and proved immensely popular with independent drivers, especially outside of the UK.

Brabham BT40

The Mathews collection has two cars from the classic car marque that is Brabham. Started by Jack Brabham in the 1960's and later owned by Formula 1 boss Bernie Ecclestone, the marque created a series of highly successful cars that competed in many different Formulae in the 1960's to the 1980's. Brabham proved to be one of the most popular and easy to run of the customer cars built by the major race car constructors during that period.

The Formula 2 Brabham BT-40 was the idea and work of Geoff Ferris and is very similar in design concept to his previous F2 car, the BT-38. The full monocoque chassis is made from 16 gauge NS4 inner and outer skins with square section steel tube bulkheads, front and rear. It has no external piping to increase the aerodynamic drag of the car, and also to allow a clear airflow to the centrally mounted radiators. The body is moulded from fiberglass with a 1/8th" thick perspex screen. A Formula 1 style rear wing, with built in curling trailing edge, is used to increase download. The four valve Cosworth BDA engine in this Formula Atlantic version of the BT40, as with the F2 model, is mounted in a tubular subframe, suspension is conventional with coil

spring damper units mounted outboard all around and the wheels are a fully machined conical design formed from magnesium alloy, with the front wheels incorporating a brake cooling system. The BT-40 has an excellent power to weight ratio and all this adds up to a wonderfully quick car with good handling that is very easy and fun to drive.

Formula Atlantic was a hotly contested North American series that helped to train driving stars such as Bobby Rahal, Keke Rosberg and Gilles Villenueve, as well as becoming popular in the UK, where drivers like Tony Brise emerged through the formula.

SPECIFICATIONS

Make: Brabham	Model: BT-40 Formula 2
Year: 1972	Color: Red
Engine: Cosworth BDP	CC: 2000
Power: 270 bhp	Transmission: Hewland FT200
Brakes: Solid Discs	Length: not available
Width: not available	Height: not available
Weight: 1100 lbs	Chassis no: BT-40-27
Drivers: n/a	

Hawke FF DL2B

During the late 1960's, the Formula Ford series was established as an economy race series with very strict guidelines. The first batch of cars built by Lotus Components all had to have the same 1600cc Ford engine and transmission, putting the emphasis on the driver. Formula Ford quickly became one of the most competitive racing classes, and remains that way today.

Hawke, set up by David Lazenby, a one-time manager of Lotus Components and mechanic for the legendary racing driver Jim Clark at Indianapolis, was one of the major Formula Ford producers in the late 1960's and early 1970's. He created the Hawke marque to build cars for the smaller race series (after the failure of Lotus' first excursion into Formula Ford) and they went on to win the manufacturers championship in 1972. Lazenby's first creation was the Hawke DL-1, which in 1969 became the DL-2 production car. In total, thirty five DL-2s, 2As and 2Bs were built over two seasons. The DL2B is built from a multi-tubular spaceframe, with a fiberglass cockpit cowling, undertray and a separate nose and tail.

The DL-2A sold well and Hawke grew, until Lazenby over stretched his resources and almost went out of business. He was helped out by Mac McKinstry and Hawke recovered and built the popular DL-12, but because of the oil crisis, orders dropped and the marque was again in trouble. Mike Keegan, the head of British Air Ferries and sponsor of his son Rupert's Formula Ford efforts, bought a controlling share of Hawke and set about designing a F3 car. Again Hawke had survived but Lazenby had tired of the

internal politics of the company and sold his remaining shares in 1978. Keegan did not last long after Lazenby's departure and the doors at Hawke finally shut in August 1979.

The Hawke marque is quintessential English Formula Ford and the DL 2B was its most successful championship winning car.

SPECIFICATIONS

Make: Hawke	Model: DL2B Formula Ford
Year: 1972	Color: Blue
Engine: Ford 4 Cylinder	CC: 1600
Power: 114 bhp	Transmission: Hewland 4 speed
Brakes: Discs	Length: 142"
Width: 63"	Height: 38"
Weight: 1050 lbs	Chassis no: unknown
Drivers: n/a	

Ferrari 365GTB4

The 365 GTB/4 was produced by Ferrari between 1969 and 1974, and in those five years, less than 1284 coupes were built. The initial reaction at the launch was mixed, there was disappointment that Ferrari had not built a car in direct competition to the mid-engined Lamborghini Miura. The 365 GTB/4 was given the nickname Daytona by journalists after Ferrari's amazing 1-2-3 victory at the Daytona 24 hour race which finally broke the complete dominance of the Ford GT40s.

The 94.5" wheelbase dates back to the 250GT SWB of 1959.

Designed by Fioravanti of Pininfarina, the Daytona is an all time classic shape with a long nose, short cabin and a stumpy cut off tail. With no additions to the outside to ruin its lines the sleek streamlining also gives the body extra stability at speed. No pressing tools were made for the body so all of the curves and sweeping lines had to be formed around a master wooden buck. The pieces were then welded together on a jig to maintain accuracy, although exact replication was impossible; the Daytona looks mass produced but no two are exactly the same.

The Daytona's 60 degree, 4.4 litre V12 engine was designed by Aurelio Lampredi, it helped to make the Daytona the fastest production car of the day with a maximum speed of 174 mph. Autocar tested the Daytona at MIRA proving ground in the UK in 1971 and managed to get 0-60 in 5.4 seconds, 0-100 in a spectacular 12.6 seconds and 0-130 in 21.5. It also managed the incredible feat of reaching 150 mph within the one mile straight at MIRA - no other car was capable of this. The engine was based on the 275 GTB twin cam, but was a new unit created in part to meet increasingly rigid emission regulations. The engine is set well back in the tubular frame creating the near perfect weight ratio of 52% front to 48% rear.

The Daytona was the last of the great front engined V12 Berlinettas and could be viewed as the ultimate, most macho of all the Ferrari GTs; the culmination of a bloodline that goes back to the 275 and 250 and Ferrari's first road cars. The Daytona is based on the same chassis as the 275 GTB/4, they also shares the same double wishbone/coil independent front and rear suspension and five speed gear trans-axle located in a unit within the rear axle.

The Mathews Daytona is completely original and has never been restored. It has 35,000 miles on the clock and was initially owned by a Colorado business man who had it from new. The Daytona is a real driving experience with large quantities of power available. The wonderful sound of the V12 engine makes the inclusion of a radio superfluous. With its heavy steering the Daytona is not really a city car and is best suited to the open road.

SPECIFICATIONS

Make: Ferrari	Model: 365 GTB-4 Daytona
Year: 1972	Color: Red
Engine: V12 quad cam	CC: 4390
Power: 352 bhp	Transmission: 5 speed manual
Brakes: Discs	Length: 174"
Width: 69"	Height: 49"
Weight: 3600 lbs	Chassis no: 14599
Drivers: n/a	

Ferrari 365GTC4

The 365 GTC4 is one of the finest and most underrated cars that Ferrari ever produced. Only about 500 were built in the 365 GTC4's production run between the spring of 1971 and the autumn of 1972. The GTC is short for Grand Turismo Coupe, indicating that the car was never going to be the most exciting car in the Ferrari stable, but it was built more as a luxury car specifically for the American market. The 365 GTC4 is often called the 'forgotten Ferrari' as it is not as popular as most Ferraris but it marked a watershed in their design. The rounded curves gave way to sharply defined edges and it is not as aggressively styled as the Daytona.

The interior was typically stark with the dashboard made up from big white on black instruments. There were no external mirrors to ruin the sleek look of the 365 GTC4 but visibility was still good through the rear window. The car came with air conditioning, electric windows and more importantly, power steering which add to the luxury of the car. The power steering adds so much to the driving experience that it takes the 365 GTC4 into the realms of Ferraris other great touring cars.

The 365 GTC4 engine is the same capacity and has the same bottom half as the Daytona, but from there on is completely different. The lower hood line required new cylinder heads to be built with new intake manifolds mounted between the camshafts. Another difference is that the five speed transmission is integral with the engine rather than mounted at the rear as in the Daytona. The American 'open road' is where this car was designed for and where it performs best.

SPECIFICATIONS

Make: Ferrari	Model: 365GTC4
Year: 1972	Color: Brown
Engine: V12 quad cam	CC: 4390
Power: 330 bhp	Transmission: 5 speed manual
Brakes: Discs	Length: 176"
Width: 69"	Height: 48"
Weight: 3600 lbs	Chassis no: 15613
Drivers: n/a	

Corvette Anniversary & Pacecar

To mark the Corvette's silver anniversary, Chevrolet had the most significant redesign since 1968. The 1978 Corvette had new fastback rear styling, creating more passenger space and a larger rear window. The interior was also modernized, the speedometer and tachometer were redesigned in a new squarer more vertical style and a glove box was added. On the exterior, all 1978 Corvettes had a '25th Anniversary' emblem.

1978 was not only Corvette's 25th birthday but also the first time they paced the Indy 500. To celebrate the event, Chevrolet built a series of pace car replicas. Chevrolet were extremely proud of the fact that as a pace car the Corvette was the first car to use a completely stock drivetrain, the first to be built from a one piece fiberglass body and the only pure two seater since before the beginning of World War II. These pace car replicas had their own VIN or Vehicle Identification Number, separate from the standard Corvette, another first for the marque. The difference between the VIN number for the standard Corvette and pace car replica is in the eighth digit, the pace car replica has a 9, the Corvette a 4. As

well as having their own identification, the pace car replicas had their own paint scheme which consisted of a two tone paint with a red stripe. The first 300 pace car replicas had tires specially made by Goodyear with 'Corvette' imprinted on the side. The extremely high demand for the pace car continually increased the quantity produced and in the end Chevrolet decided to build one for every Corvette dealer, a total of 6,502.

The pace car paint scheme evolved into a special "Silver Anniversary" paint option. The Silver Anniversary Corvette has a lighter silver upper and darker silver lower body surface which is split up with silver striping; on these cars, sport mirrors and aluminum wheels were added. There was no limit imposed on the quantity of Silver Anniversary cars produced and the total tally was 15,283

OFFICIAL

62nd ANNUAL INDIANAPOLIS 500

SPECIFICATIONS

Make: Chevrolet	Model: Corvette
Year: 1978	Color: Black & Silver, Silver
Engine: Chevrolet V8	CC: 5735
Power: 220 bhp	Transmission: 3 speed auto
Brakes: Discs	Length: 185"
Width: 69"	Height: 48"
Weight: 3000 lbs	Chassis no: 1Z8748S425809
Drivers: n/a	

Ferrari 550

The 550 Maranello is Ferrari's up to the minute interpretation of the great front engined V-12 berlinettas of the last century. The 550 has been built in the great Ferrari tradition and does not concede anything to driveability and comfort.

The 550's aerodynamics were shaped in the wind tunnel. The hours of testing have made sure that there is minimum drag and a constant vertical load on the wheels regardless of the car's set up. The body was designed by Pininfarina who, once again, has produced a great sports car that is low and wide with a cut off tail. Styling details include the air intake which is positioned low and incorporates the foglights at either end. The two hot air outlet bays in the front fender, between the door and wheel arch, are a design reference back to the great front engined Ferraris such as the 250GTO. The rear end of the car has been left simple, it rises in the middle where a small spoiler links it to the roof. The tail includes the characteristic Ferrari double lights.

The 550 is laid out in a classical way with the engine in the front, powering the rear wheels. The 550 engine is a 12 cylinder 65°V and weighs

SPECIFICATIONS

Make: Ferrari	Model: 550 Maranello
Year: 2001	Color: Silver
Engine: 12 Cylinder	CC: 5473
Power: 485 bhp	Transmission: 6 speed syncro
Brakes: Discs	Length: 180"
Width: 76"	Height: 50"
Weight: 3726 lbs	Chassis no: ZFF2S49A610122689
Drivers: n/a	

518 lbs, the chassis is a tubular steel frame with the light aluminum bodywork welded to it, the gearbox is positioned at the rear for better weight distribution. The whole thing runs on low pressure cast magnesium wheels which are controlled by independent suspension. This suspension incorporates shock absorbers that have both a normal and a sports setting that can be changed between by the driver with the flick of a switch on the dashboard. The ZF rack and pinion steering comes with Servotronic speed sensitive power steering. The fuel tank holds 30 US gallons and is formed from a light aluminum alloy.

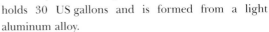

Porsche 924GTS

The Porsche 924 Carrera GTS is an unusual car, as a thinly disguised Group 4 car it is a fun, fast and lightweight factory built car. Work began on Porsche's first ever front engined, water cooled car, the 924 in 1972. The idea to modify the 924 originated with the production of the Porsche 924 GT which was designed for Group 4 (modified production car) racing. In 1981 Porsche began

SPECIFICATIONS

Make: Porsche	Model: 924 Carrera GTS Club Sport
Year: 1981	Color: Red
Engine: 4 Cylinder Turbo	CC: 1984
Power: 270 bhp	Transmission: 5 speed manual
Brakes: Discs	Length: 164"
Width: 69"	Height: 50"
Weight: 2200 lbs	Chassis no: WPO2229322B710017
Drivers: n/a	

building the GTS and the Mathews car is number seventeen of only fifty nine cars that Porsche homologised for Le Mans 24 hour race. It is made ever scarcer by the fact that this is one of only fifteen of the these that were fitted with 270 bhp engines. The factory Porsche 924s did well at Le Mans in 1981 and finished an extremely respectable seventh overall.

To make the necessary weight savings required for racing, Porsche had to make extensive modifications between the standard 924 and the GTS version. The front fenders and rear bumper extensions

are formed from fiberglass. The wafer thin doors and hood are made from lightweight aluminum, in fact only the bare necessities - the sills and roof - are made from steel. Other pointers to the GTS's race pedigree is that it sits a lot closer to the ground than the standard car and the usual 924 retractable headlights are replaced with these slat shaped lights. Porsche also tried to save as much weight as possible in the cockpit. The windows have no winding mechanism, instead the perspex windows are operated by manually sliding them. There is also a bare minimum of carpet. Obviously for safety reasons, the weight saving did not go as far as the seats which are huge, rally style. All the weight savings added to the power of the Porsche 4 Cylinder Turbo engine that gave almost double the power of the stock 924. The 2 litre SOHC four engine is fitted with an air to air intercooler and can produce 245 bhp at 6,250 rpm and 245 pounds-feet of torque at 3,000 rpm. The power is controlled by a standard 924 5 speed manual gearbox but it is modified with a separate oil cooler and a 40% limited slip differential.

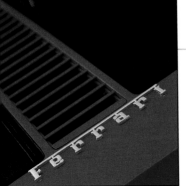

Ferrari 512BBi

Designed by Pininfarina and built by Scaglietti, the mid engined Boxer was the successor to the front engined V12 Daytona. The original Boxer, known as the 365GT4 BB was first shown at the Turin Motor Show in 1971 but did not go on sale until 1974. Introduced at the Paris Salon in 1976, the 512 BB superseded the 365 GT4 BB; its engine was enlarged from 4390 cc to 4942 cc, although the horse power dropped from 380 bhp at 7000 rpm in the 365 GT4 BB to 360 bhp at 6200 rpm to meet noise and emission regulations, particularly in the USA. The 512 BB body varied little from its predecessor, although the rear-end was widened to accommodate new wider tires and two sets of rear lights replaced the previous six. The six exhaust pipes were replaced by two double exhausts and a new spoiler was added at the front under the grille. The new engine and tires made the 512 BB a much more driveable car. In 1981 the 512 BB was replaced by the fuel injected, but otherwise almost identical 512 BBi. This model proved to be the most popular and 1007 were built until production ended in 1984.

The 512 BB designation can be broken down; the 5 indicates the displacement, although it is actually just under at 4942cc, the 12 represents the number of cylinders that are capable of producing 360 bhp. The first B is for Berlinetta, which is essentially a closed coupe, the second B stands for Boxer.

The name 'Boxer' comes from the engine which is vertically opposed, meaning the cylinders are arranged in a flat configuration and opposed to each other by 180 degrees. This was the first time Ferrari had used a Boxer engine in a road going car and the Flat 12 made it possible to mount the engine above the transmission, which allowed the space to create a better driving position. The Boxer engine was extremely powerful giving a top speed of 188 mph, 0-60 in 5.5 seconds and 0-100 in just 13.2 seconds. The positioning of the engine also added to handling, the centralized weight allowing for faster cornering.

The car is built around a tubular steel frame which holds the engine, transmission, steering and suspension components. The cabin is made of steel, the lower body panels are formed from

SPECIFICATIONS

Make: Ferrari	Model: 512 BBi
Year: 1984	Color: Red
Engine: Flat 12	CC: 4942
Power: 360 bhp	Transmission: 5 speed manual
Brakes: Servo asst Discs	Length: 173"
Width: 72"	Height: 44"
Weight: 3465 lbs	Chassis no: 2FFJA09B000051073
Drivers: n/a	

fiberglass and the nose and tail are clothed in alloy clamshells. The panel joints are all obvious, with no attempt made to hide them. The suspension is wishbone all around with twin coil springs at the rear and the steering is rack and pinion. All of the details and mechanics add to the pure race driving experience.

When designing the Boxer, Pininfarina did away with years of Ferrari design that had culminated in the Daytona and created a true racing car for the road. The Daytona looked back, the Boxer forward to a new era of mid-engined supercars. The Boxer was low slung and racy and was in direct competition with the mid-engined Lamborghini Miura, but Ferrari's had their racing heritage and experience with the 312PB that had dominated the 1972 Sports Car Championship to draw from and this gave the Boxer the edge on its competition. The racing influence is carried into the interior which is spartan. The car is designed and built around the driver and heightening their experience, thus leaving little storage space.

The 512 BBi in the Mathews collection was one of the last of this model to be built and Harry often uses it as his personal transport. The air conditioning, power windows and central locking doors which come as standard all helping to make it an easy car for everyday use. The 512 BB is fine for normal speeds but does not really come alive until it is allowed to reach velocity. The acceleration is incredibly quick and with the engine just behind the drivers head, motoring becomes a multi sensorial experience.

Corvette Pacecar & ZR1

1986/1991

1986 was the second opportunity for Corvette to provide the Official Pace Car for the Indianapolis 500, where the car was driven by famous test pilot Chuck Yeager. Chevrolet were proud because they did not need to make any modifications to their car for this task. This meant that all 7,315 convertibles, no matter what their specification or color scheme, are considered Pace Car replicas. It was also the first convertible Corvette since 1975.

The 1986 Corvette was introduced to the world at the Detroit Auto Show with its ABS braking system which became standard equipment with all 1986 Corvettes. The new brakes worked through a system of sensors at each wheel that transferred data to a computerized electronic control unit. A center line "High Mount" stoplight was added to the 1986 Corvette to comply with federal requirements. On the convertible, the light was inserted into the rear facia.

The highly anticipated ZR1 Corvette was introduced in 1990 and became known as "The King of the Hill". It was to be the fastest ever Corvette with an approximate maximum speed of 180 mph, doing 0-60 in 4.2 seconds making it the quickest accelerating production car in the world. Everything in the car, including driveability, performance and the need to meet federal emission and mileage rules, are computer controlled. The ZR1

was the most expensive GM car ever made but compared to other supercars of the time, it was comparatively cheap.

The thing that makes the ZR1 special is its engine, the LT5, designed by Lotus. The incredibly complex V8 all alloy engine was based on the standard Corvette engine configuration but was improved by the addition of four overhead camshafts operating four valves per cylinder, giving a grand total of 32 valves. The LT5 engine is boosted by its air intake system that can either take oxygen form a single narrow throttle valve or from a wide mouth intake depending on the pressure applied to the accelerator. The engines were manufactured and assembled by Mercury Marine.

The 1991 model has some design differences from the 1990 ZR1, including restyled rear exterior with four rectangular tail lights. Changes to the front consisted of wrap around parking, cornering and fog lights. Although they looked similar, the 1991 ZR1 had new door and rear body panels to accommodate the new wider 11 inch rear wheels. The ZR1 in the Mathews collection has only travelled a total of 825 miles.

Make: Chevrolet	Model: Corvette
Year: 1986	Color: Yellow
Engine: Chevrolet V8	CC: 5700
Power: 240 bhp	Transmission: 4 speed manual
Brakes: Discs	Length: 176.5"
Width: 71"	Height: 47"
Weight: 3100 lbs	Chassis no: 1G1YY6782G5902682
Drivers: n/a	

Make: Chevrolet	Model: ZR1 Corvette
Year: 1991	Color: Metallic Turquoise
Engine: Lotus LT5 V8	CC: 5735
Power: 375 bhp	Transmission: ZF Six speed manual
Brakes: Discs	Length: 178.5"
Width: 71"	Height: 47"
Weight: 3465 lbs	Chassis no: 1G1YZ23J7M5801227
Drivers: n/a	

Corvette '95 & '98 Pace, Gran Sport

1995 was the third year for Corvette to pace the Indianapolis 500 with the Pace Car, on this occasion, driven by Chevrolet General Manager Jim Perkins. His car was powered by a stock 300 bhp LT1 V8 engine with automatic transmission and painted with a dark metallic accent over an arctic white bottom half and a white convertible top. To celebrate the event Chevrolet announced on the 3rd of January that it would be producing a limited run of 527 convertible pace car replicas.

The LT1 was introduced by Chevrolet as the Corvette engine in 1992, replacing the L98. All of the road-going 1995 Pace Car replicas had the LT1 engine, with either 300 or 340 bhp ratings. Improvements were made to the strength of the engine in 1995 by changing the connecting rods to a powered metal design.

The 1995 Pace Car replicas all came complete with purple and white paint work, reflecting the Perkins Car. They also came complete with special Indy Pace Car exterior graphics and internally the black leather sport bucket seats were embroidered with the 79th Indianapolis 500 logo. Styling wise, the 1996 Corvette was only distinguished from the 1995 model by changes to the front fender air vents.

The 1996 Corvette Grand Sport was built to commemorate the sports car racers of the mid 1960s with the same name; it is painted Admiral Blue with a central white strip in homage to them. 1996 was the last year of the body style and the Grand Sport was meant as a 'swansong'. A limited edition of about 400 coupe were built as Grand Sports.

All 1996 Corvettes had the option of being fitted with Chevrolet's new small block LT4 engine. The new engine is basically a super LT1 with high flow heads, new cam and pistons providing the additional 300 bhp that was possible with the LT4 5.7 litre V8 engine. The LT4 engine was only available with manual transmission.

SPECIFICATIONS

Make: Chevrolet	Model: Corvette	Make: Chevrolet	Model: Corvette Grand Sport	Make: Chevrolet	Model: Corvette
Year: 1995	Color: Purple and white	Year: 1996	Color: Blue with white stripe	Year: 1998	Color: Blue and yellow
Engine: Chevrolet V8	CC: 5735	Engine: Chevrolet LT4	CC: 5735	Engine: Chevrolet V8	CC: 5735
Power: 300 bhp	Transmission: 4 speed auto	Power: 330 bhp	Transmission: 6 speed manual	Power: 345 bhp	Transmission: 6 speed manual
Brakes: Discs	Length: 178.5"	Brakes: Discs	Length: 178.5"	Brakes: Discs	Length: 180"
Width: 71"	Height: 46"	Width: 71"	Height: 46"	Width: 74"	Height: 48"
Weight: 3225 lbs	Chassis no: 1G1YY327S5113308	Weight: 3220 lbs	Chassis no: 1G1YY2255T5600030	Weight: 3218lbs	Chassis no: 1G1YY32G6W5118713
Drivers: n/a		Drivers: n/a		Drivers: n/a	

starts at the engine vent and extends the length of the doors. The rear of the body flows up into the top of the four tail lights. The new design is easier to get into and out of than previous models. Corvette has managed to maintain the low and lean look, keep the frame rigid and the entry ways open. The increased ease of use is continued to the new hood which pivots from the front end, allowing easier access to the engine.

The Corvette is the ultimate American car and Harry Mathews' love of them is reflected in his collection. All of his Corvettes have low mileage and are kept immaculate.

1998 was the fourth time Corvette paced the Indy 500, with golfer Greg Norman driving the convertible pace car. Chevrolet went on to build 1100 pace car replicas to commemorate the event and the Mathews car is one of only about 200 of these that are fitted with a 6 speed manual transmission. The Pace Car replica is painted purple and fitted with a black and yellow leather interior.

The 1998 convertible Corvette is the first convertible version of the fifth generation Corvette, the C5. The main differences from its predecessors are a re-engineered chassis and a more powerful all aluminum engine. Other changes are two plastic access panels, one opens onto a 13.9 cubic foot trunk (the first time since 1962 that the Corvette had a separate trunk with outside access) , the other conceals the stowed top. The top is a manual fold down design, eliminating the need for a large and complex system for a power top. The manual fold top is easy to use and once complete, is lowered out of sight behind the seats.

The new design has made the 1998 Corvette wider and lower than its predecessors. New styling includes an indentation that

The Bikes

Indian Chief

"The most popular bike of its time"

The Indian Motocycle Company began producing their first, single cylinder motorcycles in 1902, becoming one of the first motorcycle brands, not only in the USA, but in the world. The company was formed by Oscar Hedstrom and George Hendee and with Hedstrom's engineering skills and Hendee's business abilities, their company soon started to flourish. Indian Motocycles were ground breakers, for example the Hendee Special built in 1913 was the first ever motorcycle with electric start and a fully modern electrical system. Before the outbreak of World War 1, Hedstrom and Hendee built Indian up to be the largest motorcycle manufacturer in the world, producing over 20,000 bikes per year.

The Chief was introduced in 1922 as Indian's top of the range model. It was based on the Indian Scout frame but had a larger 61 Cubic Inch V-Twin engine; the added power gave the Chief instant appeal to consumers and was an immediate success. The larger 74 Cubic Inch engine was introduced in 1923 and in 1940 the trademark full skirted guards appeared. The Chief was at its most popular between 1946-48 due to the post war boom but by 1949 the factory considered it obsolete and

there was no Chief for that year. The Chief's absence did not last long and it was back by popular demand in 1950 although production finally ceased in 1953.

The 1947 Indian Chief shown has a 74 ci flathead engine with 3 speed transmission, a left-hand tank shift and left side foot clutch. This was the first year that Indian introduced the head fender light and for the first time the left hand shifter/right hand throttle was offered as a factory option.

SPECIFICATIONS

Make: Indian	Model: Chief
Year: 1947	Color: Red & black
Engine: V-Twin	CC: 1212
Power: 51 bhp	Transmission: 3 speed
Brakes: Drum	Length: 93"
Width: 37"	Height: 40"
Weight: 675 lbs	Chassis no: 3476041
Drivers: n/a	

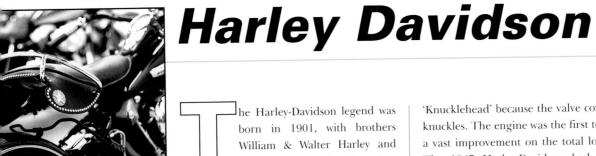

The Harley-Davidson legend was born in 1901, with brothers William & Walter Harley and Arthur Davidson in Milwaukee, Wisconsin USA. Production began in 1903 when they built a grand total of three bikes, but these creations, made with borrowed tools and metal, were different from any other motor-bikes at the time. They had a loop frame, a design that was unique to them, and were powered by a tiny three horsepower engine. By 1920 Harley-Davidson had become the largest motorbike manufacturer in the world with dealers in 67 countries. In that year sales rose by a staggering 5000 percent.

The 'Knucklehead' engine was introduced in 1936 and the 1947 Harley-Davidson EL 74 was the last bike to use it. The name was given to the engine by bikers who christened it 'Knucklehead' because the valve covers looked like a fist with two knuckles. The engine was the first to use an oil circulation system, a vast improvement on the total loss system of previous models. The 1947 Harley-Davidson had a new handshift four-speed transmission and a 'suicide clutch' which was operated by foot. It was the only civilian Harley-Davidson OHV to use the straight leg frame until its re-introduction after the Second World War in 1954. The 1947 Harley-Davidson with its wrap-around oil tank, rounded teardrop gas tank and many chrome accessories was a revelation in motorbike engineering.

SPECIFICATIONS

Make: Harley Davidson	Model: EL
Year: 1947	Color: Dark Red
Engine: V Twin	CC: 1212
Power: 51 bhp	Transmission: 4 speed
Brakes: Drum	Length: 92"
Width: 37"	Height: 42"
Weight: 650 lbs	Chassis no: 1947EL4363
Drivers: n/a	

Bantam

The 1955 BSA Bantam, or model type D1, is the smallest of all the motorcycles in the Mathews Collection and is a pertinent example of early British bikes.

The BSA Bantam was one of the most successful lightweight bikes ever to be built in the UK. BSA launched the D1 in March 1948 and the first production bike was ready in June of that year. The D1 was originally only built for export but by October it was given the name Bantam and introduced to the home market. Incredibly, BSA continued to manufacture the Bantam with various upgrades and model changes until 1971, although production in D1 specification ceased in 1963.

change that was made was to convert the dimensions from centimetres to inches so the BSA factory could work on the mechanics with ease.

The first Bantam models were made from a rigid welded steel tube frame, with simple telescopic undamped front forks. The mudguards are distinctively large, especially at the back, and the front carries a number plate on both sides. The Bantam's original price tag was £60, and for that money the 123cc 4.5 bhp engine gave a top speed of around 50 mph and an extremely economic 120 mpg. After 1950, BSA made some changes for the better, giving the Bantam a new generator, a new stand and other minor mechanics that all added to the driveability of the bike.

All Bantams were painted almost entirely in Mist Green, except for the cream colored panels on the sides of the petrol tank, which showed the BSA name. The transfers with the logo were originally the simple, yet well known, BSA 'flying wing' but on later bikes, like this one in the Mathews Collection, the image was changed to incorporate the word Bantam and the picture of a rooster.

SPECIFICATIONS

Make: BSA	Model: Bantam
Year: 1955	Color: Mist Green
Engine: Single cylinder	CC: 123
Power: 4.5 bhp	Transmission: 3 speed
Brakes: Drums	Length: 79"
Width: 31"	Height: 40"
Weight: 250 lbs	Chassis no: BD36134
Drivers: n/a	

The Bantam was not in fact a British design but was actually an almost exact copy of German manufacturer DKW's RT125. DKW were highly instrumental in the evolution of two stroke technology and after the Second World War the DKW designs were taken over as part of the war reparations. The major problem this caused BSA was that the gear change and kick-start were, as they are on European bikes, both on the left hand side of the bike and of course they needed them on the right for use in Britain. The answer to this problem was simple, BSA merely flipped all the design drawings, creating a mirror image of the original DKW RT125. One other significant

Edward Turner conceived the Square Four engine in 1928. Turner would later go on to design the Triumph twin and become the head of the Triumph Company, but at this time he was looking for work, taking drawings of his revolutionary engine around the motorcycle industry. The idea for the engine, which was comprised of a pair of 'across the frame' parallel twins linked by a pair of gears, was adopted by Ariel, then very much a force in the British motorcycle industry. The engine had its problems but in theory was almost a perfect motor, compact and well balanced.

The prototype was a 500cc capacity engine, so well contained that it fitted into the frame of the Ariel 250. The basic design was worked on and a modified version was released in 1930. It caused a massive stir, and as it was ideal for sidecar riders, an upgraded 600 cc version was released in 1932 specifically for this purpose.

In 1937 the Square Four went through a complete redesign. The old engine had been fitted with an overhead camshaft that had led to the engine's major weakness – a tendency to overheat around the cylinder head. The 1937 engine replaced the camshafts with pushrods and the crank and crankcase were

completely changed. A 1000cc option was added to the standard 600cc for the first time. Production ceased during the War and afterwards only the 1000cc model was built and offered with telescopic forks. In 1949 the engine became all alloy and the overall handling and acceleration improved.

The Square Four 4G MK II seen here, was built between 1953 and 1958. It had multiple engine upgrades from the original and other changes included four separate exhaust pipes. It was an incredible machine, the Square Four engine combined with the expansive 1000cc capacity to give a super bike, that had by far the largest British engine available at the time.

SPECIFICATIONS

Make: Ariel	Model: 4G MK II
Year: 1955	Color: Black
Engine: Sqaure Four	CC: 997
Power: 42 bhp	Transmission: 4 speed
Brakes: Drum	Length: 82"
Width: 32"	Height: 44"
Weight: 460 lbs	Chassis no: GL439
Drivers: n/a	

Nortons

The 500T was the first purpose built trials bike that Norton produced. Introduced in 1949 the 500T was first shown at the 1948 Earls Court Show and was the result of two years work. The new model came with a 500cc overhead valve engine fitted into a modified 16H frame. The rigid frame had a shorter wheelbase and redesigned steering geometry. The total weight of the 500T was kept down to only 320 lbs by replacing the iron cylinder head and barrel with a new alloy version. The 500T had no lights or dynamo and with 7.5 inches of ground clearance it all added up to be a highly competitive and successful trials bike. It was dropped from the Norton range in 1954 when they were taken over by AMC.

The Norton Commando was introduced in 1967 at the Earls Court Show to high acclaim. This model, with a 750cc engine, was built until April 1973 when the 850cc model was launched. The new 850cc engine had similar power to its predecessor, but with more torque was less stressed and thus provided more reliability.

The Norton Commando engine had its origins in the Model 7 Twin 497cc engine designed by Bert Hopwood. The engine grew in capacity via its various incarnations in the 650cc Dominator and the 745cc Atlas, to its place in the 750cc Commando. The most revolutionary part of the Commando is its frame, which was the idea of engineer Dr. Stefan Bauer. He had previously worked at Rolls Royce and believed that the standard frame design went against all engineering principals; his solution was a bike designed around a single 2.25" top tube. Bauer also wanted to free the bike from violent vibrations; to do this, the engine, gearbox and swingarm assembly were bolted together and isolated from the frame by special rubber mountings. This eliminated the extreme vibration problems that were apparent in other models in the range, as it effectively separated the driver from the engine.

The Norton Commando was an incredibly popular motorcycleand it deservedly won the MCN Machine of the Year for five successive years between 1968-1972. Some regard it as the British Motorcycle Industry's swansong, selling well right from its introduction in '67 through to the effective end of the British bike industry in the mid 1970's.

SPECIFICATIONS

Make: Norton	Model: 500T GP
Year: 1950	Colour: Silver
Engine: Twin	CC: 500
Power: 65 bhp	Transmission: 4 speed
Brakes: Drum	Length: 77"
Width: 20"	Height: 43"
Weight:285 lbs	Chassis no: 91293

Make: Norton	Model: Commando
Year: 1974	Color: Red
Engine: Twin	CC: 829
Power: 60 bhp	Transmission: 4 speed
Brakes: Drum	Length: 57"
Width: 36"	Height: 31"
Weight: 460 lbs	Chassis no: 811812

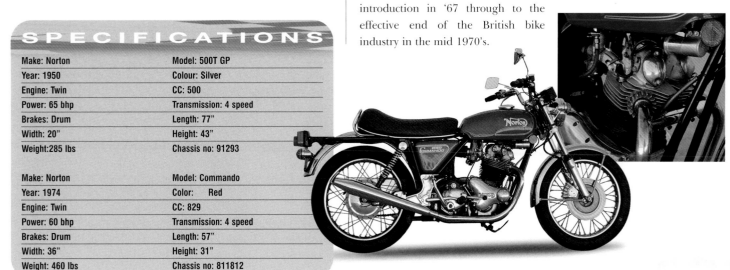

Triumph TR6

Triumph Engineering Company were based in Coventry, England. They built their first motorcycle in 1902 and in 1906 they introduced a 3 bhp bike with magneto ignition. The forerunner to the TR6 was the 500 cc TR5 which was designed for rugged sporting events and easily adaptable to most forms of motorbike competition. The TR6 was introduced as an upgrade to the TR5 with a larger engine to provide the additional power and speed required for some events.

The TR6 engine is a overhead valve high compression vertical twin with two gear driven camshafts with dry sump lubrication, pressure fed big ends and valve gear. It also had a new alloy cylinder head. The exhaust pipe is an upswept two into one with silencer. The frame is a brazed cradle type with swing arm rear suspension.

SPECIFICATIONS

Make: Triumph	Model: TR6
Year: 1956	Color: Blue and Black
Engine: Two Cylinder	CC: 649
Power: 42 bhp	Transmission: 4 speed
Brakes: Drums	Length: 85.5"
Width: 28.5"	Height: 31"
Weight: 370 lbs	Chassis no: not available

56 TR6

BSA Sport Star

The BSA Sports Star is a sport tuned version of the BSA C15 that was added to the BSA range in 1961. The C15 was introduced in 1958 as the replacement for the disastrous C12, with a redesigned frame and a new engine. The new C15 was instantly successful with its modern, clean uncluttered appearance which followed in the true tradition of British motorcycling.

The C15 engine was based on the Triumph Tiger Cub 200 cc but with a vertical cylinder. For the first time, the C15 combined the engine and gearbox as a 'Unit Single', making maintenance easier and improving reliability. The Sports Star engine was the same as a C15 but tuned for better performance with a compression rate of 10:1, although in 1962 this was lowered to 8.75:1. To cope with this extra power, a forged steel flywheel replaced the cast iron one from the C15 and caged double roller big ends were also fitted. The handlebars were lowered to further enhance the sleeker, sportier look. The suspension on both the C15 and Sports Star is a hydraulically damped telescopic fork at the front and a pivoted fork at the rear.

The 250cc engine was good at low speeds and gave excellent acceleration, especially in 2nd and 3rd gear. The Sports Star's top speed was between 80 and 85 mph, an improvement of about 10 mph on the standard C15, and gave about 80 mpg. With the typical teardrop tank holding just over 3 gallons of fuel this gave the bike a range of around 250 miles.

The C15 and Sport Star both proved to be very popular with the younger British motorbike riders when in 1960, 250cc became the largest size of engine on bike that they could ride without taking an official driving test.

SPECIFICATIONS

Make: BSA	Model: Sports Star
Year: 1964	Color: Red and Black
Engine: Single cylinder	CC: 249
Power: 24 bhp	Transmission: 4 speed
Brakes: Drum	Length: 78"
Width: 27"	Height: 36"
Weight: 275 lbs	Chassis no: C1542923

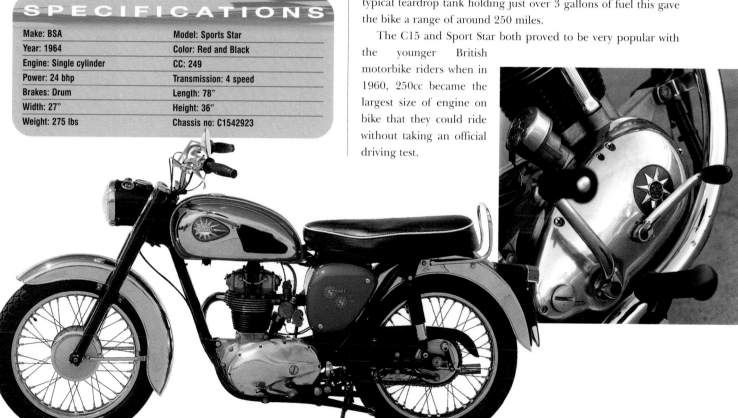

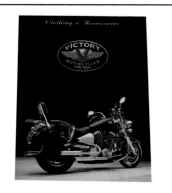

Victory & Harley Davidson

Polaris Industries Inc. introduced its 'made in the USA', large displacement cruiser motorcycles under the brand name 'Victory' in the spring of 1998, making Polaris one of the newest contenders on the motorcycle market. The brand name 'Victory' originates from the code name for the project, instead of naming it Project X, Polaris employees gave it the symbolic name Victory and it stuck.

Before the introduction of the Victory, Polaris already held a major share of the snowmobile, all terrain vehicle and personal water craft markets. They began looking into motorcycles as an extension of their business in 1993. Careful research showed Polaris that their market should be Cruisers. With over 200,000 units sold annually worldwide this sector of the market is an incredibly lucrative area for many companies.

Production of Victory's first bike, the V92C, began at Polaris' Spirit Lake, Iowa plant on July 4th, 1998, and in less than a year, by April 1999, Victory had built and shipped their first 1500 V92C motorcycles to the dealers. The V92C's engine is a fuel injected 50 degree V-Twin, displacing 1507cc. A single overhead cam operates four valves per cylinder and spent gases are routed through a free-flowing staggered dual exhaust system. Power is transmitted through a 5-speed gearbox using an "anti-jerk torque converter" system and belt drive. Other features include a six-quart oil capacity, 600 lb. dry weight and a low 28-inch saddle height. The V92C

holds five gallons of gas and runs Dunlop tires on 5-spoke aluminum wheels. For 2000, the V92C had the same engine but with uprated 300mm Brembo brakes front and rear.

Polaris claims that the V92C has the strongest frame of any cruiser on the market, using the engine as a stressed member of the frame for increased strength and rigidity. Complementing the stiff frame, beefy 45mm diameter fork tubes are used up front, with a rear suspension incorporating a stiff triangulated swingarm controlled by a single shock absorber under the seat.

Victory's styling philosophy is inspired by both the aviation and automotive industries, it is also based on research and the need to meet the public's requirements for a big motorcycle with loads of power and good looks.

The Harley Davidson Road King Classic is a cross-over model designed to fit into the space between a sports bike and a tourer. The name Road King Classic is also a description, with its strong lines and broad windscreen evoking the motorcycling of days gone by without being too over sentimental or nostalgic.

The Road King Classic has a low center of gravity allowing for optimum performance over long distances and easy maneuverability when in traffic. In contrast to the Victory, the 88ci engine is isolation mounted in the Harley Davidson touring frame with details such as the rear brake reservoir and master cylinder units being integrated. The suspension is air adjusted and the tail lights are sealed in to prevent internal condensation.

Cosmetic changes that can be made by the owner include a

detachable windscreen and the addition of a passenger pillion. The leather saddlebags, only available with the Classic, are formed from stretched leather over a hard shell, which allows for travelling in all weather conditions but maintains the style.

The Harley Davidson Heritage Classic relies on Softail suspension for its quality of ride. Underneath the seats there are two gas charged shock absorbers to help iron out any bumps that the 4 inches of rear suspension may not have been able to deal with, keeping the American love affair with the road burning brightly.

The Heritage Classic styling looks back at the 1940's and 1950's and to the archetypal uncluttered American style appealing to people's love of retro. Harley Davidson has recreated some of their past designs and proved that true classics never die. For example, the huge chrome front headlight with passing lamps is taken from the Harley Davidson 1949 Hydra Glide. The studded seats and saddlebags are also vintage Harley Davidson.

Harry and Greg use all of these modern bikes on a regular basis, to cruise out of town with their friends, relax and have fun.

SPECIFICATIONS

Make: Victory	Model: V92C	Make: Harley Davidson	Model: Heritage Classic	Make: Harley Davidson	Model: Road King Classic
Year: 1999	Color: Antaries Red	Year: 2000	Color: Black	Year: 2000	Color: Red
Engine: V Twin	CC: 1507	Engine: V Twin	CC: 1550	Engine: V Twin	CC: 1550
Power: 65 bhp	Transmission: 5 speed	Power: 70 bhp	Transmission: 5 speed	Power: 70 bhp	Transmission: 5 gears
Brakes: Discs	Length: 94"	Brakes: Discs	Length: 94"	Brakes: Discs	Length: 94"
Width: 35"	Height: 53"	Width: 34"	Height: 47"	Width: 37"	Height: 54"
Weight: 650 lbs	Chassis no: V99CB15DAZ	Weight: 710 lbs	Chassis no: 603959	Weight: 720 lbs	Chassis no: 12686

Index